REFORMERS ARISE

Calling Out a People of Dignity to Influence and Action

Dedications

A Song of Victory dedicated to the
One who gave me the *Song*

To my Treasures – Kome, Efena and
Odafe, who allowed me to *Sing*

To Reformers – Young and Old –
who are singing this *New Song* with
Boldness, Courage and Dignity

REFORMERS
ARISE

*Calling Out a People of Dignity
to Influence and Action*

Alero Ayida-Otobo

REFORMERS ARISE

Calling Out a People of Dignity to Influence and Action

First published in 2017 by
Panoma Press Ltd
48 St Vincent Drive, St Albans, Herts, AL1 5SJ UK

info@panomapress.com
www.panomapress.com

Cover design by Michael Inns
Artwork by Karen Gladwell

ISBN 978-1-784521-10-3

A CIP catalogue record for this book is available from the British Library.

This book is available online and in all good bookstores.

Contents

Acknowledgements   vii

Foreword   xi

Preface   xv

Introduction: Let the Reformers Arise   xxi

1   Reformers – A Certain Kind of People   1

2   The Reformer's Mindset   15

3   Reformers Deal with Root Causes and Provide Solutions to Deep-Seated Issues   25

4   A Good Character is Non-Negotiable   43

5   You Have to Be Good at It!   59

6   It is About Influence   71

7   Reformers Do Not Work Solo – They Collaborate   89

8   Building a New Community of Reformers   101

About the Author   115

About Incubator Africa   117

References   119

Testimonials   125

Acknowledgements

When one arrives at a destination it is only a fool that thinks he did it all by himself. The book you are holding is a culmination of a 25-year journey. On this journey I have walked with different kinds of people – teachers, 'midwives', mentors and covenant friends.

There is an ancient saying: 'When the student is ready the teacher will appear.' I thank my numerous teachers – Dr Tony Rapu, Paul Adefarasin, Arnold Ekpe, Johnny and Elizabeth Enlow. They showed up at pivotal times during this 25-year journey to ensure that I learned what I needed to learn to walk in knowledge, understanding and wisdom. There is one that stands out because she is more than a teacher, she is my friend, sister and mentor – Obii Pax Harry. I remember the many nights spent in her home trying to understand the cry in our hearts for more and our desire to see our nation transformed. She carries and lives the message of reformation.

Thank you to my fellow travellers on this journey of reformation – my covenant sisters Abby Olufeyimi, Abolaji Osime, Imo Oyewole and Toyin Matthews and my covenant brother Emmanuel Dania. We have travelled together to different nations, fought and cried together, laughed and rejoiced at small but significant wins.

To the midwives that stayed by my bedside during the dark hours making sure there was no still-birth, I say *modupe* (which means thank you in the Yoruba language). *Modupe* to Shola Kotun who travelled to Atlanta in November 2015 to spend a month with me to ensure that the new emerged, and to Gori Olusina Daniel who strengthened me with words when I needed them the most. To Fidelis Okei and Omolara Cookey, thank you for your prayers and words of encouragement.

To write a book you need space and time. My life until early 2014 was full and very busy. It was quite a noisy life. An unexpected event in April 2014 made it possible to begin a journey of decluttering my life and focusing on what is truly important – to love others and to serve. This book is an expression of love. I thank my daughter Efena for giving me time during our healing journey to write this book. I remember the mornings when she would ask, "Mama, have you done your two hours of writing?" and would not allow me to do anything else until I fulfilled my obligation. I thank my daughter Kome for being my first editor. She did great and her comments were always insightful and thought provoking. My son Odafe, thank you for the many wonderful meals you cooked, giving me time to think and edit. The last three years with the three of you have brought the clarity I need for the next season of my life. I first had to walk the journey of transformation alongside you to qualify to walk alongside others.

You also need a good measure of love and care. Thank you to my parents and siblings who have demonstrated the immeasurable value of a good family. Their love and support cannot be quantified. Thank you to my sister Gubby and my three brothers, 'the boys', Omatseyin, Abidemi and Maje Ayida. The crown goes to our amazing parents, Remi and Allison Ayida, who made us feel so loved and so adored. There was nothing they wouldn't do for us. They instilled in us good values and a love for travel. I miss my Mum.

Thank you to my volunteer readers, those who endured the reading of the initial drafts of this book. Thank you for your wise and instructive comments and counsel. Thank you to the Young Reformers who took time to participate in the survey that confirmed that the time had come for a book like this. I am amazed at what some of you have accomplished since we walked together during the Young Reformers Programme. I count it an honour to serve you.

Finally to you, my reader, thank you for allowing me to show up in your life. Without you this book would not exist. So I honour and salute you for paying the price and nurturing the desire to be a reformer. You are destined to become a history maker.

Foreword

I have gotten to know and appreciate the sharpness of who Alero Ayida-Otobo is as we have interacted over the last couple of years. Because of that it was an honour to be asked to write a foreword for her new book *Reformers Arise*. I thought to myself, well this ought to be good. Everything about Alero tells you it is going to be something well thought out, meaningful and full of substantive hope. However, nothing prepared me for the amazement I would receive upon actually reading the book. I was stunned by the brilliance of her introduction and then it only grew as the book continued. I read most of the book in one sitting of several hours as it was so engaging and on point.

Reformers Arise is a clarion calling up – to the whole continent of Africa – and Alero speaks out appropriately as a Mama to the nations. Most of the wisdom in this book is needed far beyond Africa and I strongly recommend it for anybody with a heart for reformation of their nation. This book contains the perfect mix of stories, practical steps, and perhaps most importantly, a prophetic calling up of a people into available destiny. I say available destiny because I believe we have squarely entered into an advanced stage of the kingdom age and we have an unprecedented convergence of time and spiritual resources now coming together on our behalf. I belief that it is right now Africa's time and day to arise.

Africa does not lack for potential and it is now time for that potential to be made reality. The continent is full of resources and full of passionate people. This is the beginning of a recipe for glorious success. However, the rest of the recipe ingredients must now be added to the destiny mix and the author does so in a beautiful but direct way. Reformers as defined and explained in this book must – and I believe WILL – now arise all across Africa. It will start with a few uncompromising individuals and then quickly spread like a healing virus across the continent.

This generation is now ready to count the cost of going against the currents of compromise, and is ready to see Africa step into its apogee of destiny. Courage will breed courage. Action will breed action. Radical love will breed radical love. This book is representative of the courage, action and radical love that will arise and perhaps it will even be a tipping point for it. It is full of intellectually satisfying reformation examples while not so overly stating the challenges that one is afraid to even start. This rising, courageous, and loving generation must be so much more like the biblical figure of Caleb than like his accompanying 10 spies. The 10 spies were intellectual experts in the study of the giants of the Promised Land and in doing so destroyed their own, and the people's, capacity to hope. They so focused on the challenges that they suffocated the solutions. Caleb, on the other hand, recognised the convergence of destiny of his day and set out to arise with hope filled observations and solutions. He found great grapes right under the noses of the huge giants and was furthermore able to identify the 'giants' as simply bread to be eaten.

Africa, and the nations themselves, have many, many multigenerational 'giants' that seem incapable of being dealt with. As you read this book you will feel yourself being called up into being a Caleb-style reformer. Caleb reformers don't ignore the challenges but after identifying them know how to properly apportion their capabilities. Problems are only problems if solutions refuse to show up. Darkness is only a problem if light doesn't rise and shine. As the author clearly tells us, light must first choose to be light. In other words, theoretical light must be actual light. Theoretical light that takes bribes, tells lies and participates in corruption is actually still just darkness. The time for no more tolerance with these matters is here and the reforming Calebs and Joshuas will now arise. Now actually read this book that you bought and rise to its clarion call.

Johnny Enlow
Author/Speaker/Reformer

Seven Mountain Prophecy
Seven Mountain Mantle
Rainbow God
Becoming a Superhero
Seven Mountain Renaissance

www.johnnyandelizabeth.com

Preface

Africa as a continent is daunting. You hear the word Africa and it conjures up different images to different people. Images as diverse as the malnourished baby that has only a few hours to live because his or her mother is illiterate and too poor to buy food the family needs for survival, to the opulence of 50-room mansions with a row of luxury cars parked in front of a well-manicured lawn. You have images of marauders ransacking villages, raping and killing innocent men, women and children contrasted with the beauty of the rolling hills of the savannah and the pristine beaches along the Atlantic and Pacific oceans. This is the continent that has the 'good, the bad and the really ugly'.

As a people group, Africans have been stripped of their dignity through historical injustices like slavery and apartheid; through self-inflicted unforgivable acts like corruption and extreme levels of poverty; through wars, genocide and poor leadership at every level. Each unjust act peels off yet another level of dignity.

When I think of Africa I get angry – angry at missed opportunities and dashed hopes. With each new government that comes into power the citizens have great expectations but, unfortunately, with only a few exceptions, these hopes are soon dashed. Although the exceptions are growing with Rwanda, Botswana and Ghana coming readily to mind, it is time for these exceptions to become the norm.

I often ask myself the questions: What will it take to restore the dignity of my people? What will it take to develop my beloved continent? As I get older I am beginning to doubt if I will see the fullness of the change I so desire to see. I am compelled to turn to the next generation for vision, fulfilment of dreams, solutions and commitment. Can a new army arise from amongst them that will dignify themselves through their values and acts of service, to lift up a continent from its throes of poverty and underdevelopment?

Today as I write this preface, I am wearing my *ulemu* earrings. *Ulemu* means dignity. It is time to activate a people who are ready to dignify themselves and take full responsibility for the continent of Africa. For answers to some of my questions I turned to the alumni of the Young Reformers Programme (YRP), a pilot programme established in 2013 to infuse a reformer's mindset into young people between the ages of 21 to 35. The programme also challenges them to identify a sphere of society they are passionate about, and become a solution carrier for that sphere. The YRP's objective is to activate, equip and release.

I asked the YRP alumni five questions:

1. What would you say are the main obstacles to your nation's progress to becoming a Second World nation?

2. What makes you most angry about the state of your nation?

3. If you were elected President, in one sentence, what problems would you try to solve and why?

4. Name five qualities an 'agent of change' should have in your opinion.

5. What keeps you going as a reformer? Why are you doing what you do? What in your opinion is your reward?

The Young Reformers clearly articulated the main obstacles to progress and what made them angry. There were several major issues that kept recurring:

- The lack of sacrificial leaders willing to pay the price for the people

- The level of poverty and rate of unemployment

- The level of corruption

- The lack of unity – the pursuit of individuality at the expense of the generality

- The lack of collective will and commitment

In the words of one of the reformers, *"What makes me most angry about the state of my nation is not really the challenges themselves or the failure of the government as is very commonly highlighted, but the unpreparedness, inaction and errors of the people who are supposed to be part of fixing the challenges and paving the way for that desired future."*

Their answers gave me hope. Not because they were new but because of the approach and the heart condition of those who responded. These young reformers recognise that they *are* the solutions to the problems.

"As a reformer, my motivation that keeps me going is the courage and the unshakeable belief that I can make a difference, I keep taking the risks, and pressing through regardless of the pressures of life, regardless of the difficulties. I believe my country Nigeria can be truly great!"

"I wonder what I would do if not what I am currently doing. It feels as if I would die if I don't do this; I would be physically here on earth but not really here. At some point in my life I had an identity crisis until I came to the conclusion that I am a Nigerian/African by Divine Design. And so I want to see a New Nigeria. I truly believe in building my nation by investing in her children. Will I get it right? As much as I want to see immediate results it may be an impossible expectation. But I must keep sowing the seeds and praying that the seeds will fall on good soil and eventually germinate good fruit."

Calling Out a People of Dignity to Influence and Action

"My reward is simply leaving my footprints of immense value in the sands of time concerning my nation."

There *is* a new generation arising. They recognise that a new kind of person is required to bring the desired change. Each one alluded to character traits such as integrity, trustworthiness, courage, commitment, persistence and humility which we will discuss in the chapter A Good Character is Non-Negotiable.

This book is about a certain kind of people   the reformers arising and taking responsibility for the development of the nations of Africa. Without any hesitation I wish to state that this book is for the lovers of Africa who care for the continent and are fed up with excuses and want to do *something – anything* that will bring significant change. They look normal but they are not. They cry daily.

This is about changing the songs of pain and sadness that can still be heard on this beautiful and blessed continent. It is about singing new ones – songs of hope and victory. This book is about finding the new songwriters, the new sound forgers, the new freedom fighters, the pioneers willing to forge new pathways. It is about searching, finding, activating the New Reformers and building a dignified, undaunted army.

Let the Reformers Arise

This book is *a cry from the heart to see* the emergence of a new kind of people. Some call them a New Tribe. I call them a Certain Kind of People – *The Reformers*. They are young (in age and at heart), they are full of creative energy, passion and certain qualities that distinguish and differentiate them. They are tired of the status quo, tired of the state of their nations and they do not want to grow old in the same social and environmental conditions that their parents grew up in. They are like *you* – they want to see change and are willing to pay the price to be the instigator of that change.

This book is *a manual of the qualities of this certain kind of people*. It is a manual for developing, refining and releasing them. What do they look like? How do they behave? What do they do? How do they do it? Together we will explore the process of preparing this certain kind of people. Although there is a process to the preparation, what I call 'the fundamentals' – the fundamentals of becoming a reformer – each person experiences this process differently. Each person is unique and wonderfully made so the pattern and the process of becoming a reformer is as diverse. There are signposts you need to recognise even as you go through your process. We will highlight and discuss some of these signposts.

This book is also the *release of a sound*. Sound is powerful. It has the power to shatter. When a new sound comes it shatters the old, it causes a shift. The intention of this book is to cause a shift in a new generation of young people who are determined to do something meaningful with their lives. They are solution carriers and they are tired of 'band-aid' solutions that have no impact. Their solutions have the potential to be game changers. They know that if they don't do it no one else will. Martin Luther King Jr puts it this way, *"We were each chosen for a particular, cosmically important task that can be done by no-one else."* This is what makes reformers history makers.

If they do nothing, their organisations, their communities and their nations will need to wait for another community of change makers. The question is, can we afford to wait? My answer is no. What is yours? If it is no then this book is for you. You are the change that *Change* is waiting for.

Reformer – arise and take your place.

I first heard the phrase 'Reformers Arise' in 2007 at a History Makers Course in Ukraine. The two words suddenly popped into my consciousness as I reflected on why I was in Ukraine and what I was to do next. I have spent the last decade thinking about these two words. My reflections and study have led to this book. Its focus is on raising reformers in Africa. You may ask Why Africa? There are two main reasons.

Paul Collier in his book *The Bottom Billion: Why the Poorest Countries are Failing and What Can Be Done About It* highlights the countries caught in poverty traps. He mentions four of these traps: the conflict trap; the natural resources trap; the trap of being landlocked with bad neighbours; and the trap of bad governance. Unfortunately most Africans are living in countries that have been in one or another of these traps and his research shows that 70% of the people in the bottom billion are in Africa. Africa is therefore the core of the problem.

The second reason is personal – I am African and I desperately want to witness the emergence of a New Africa.

Chapter 1 examines the distinguishing qualities of reformers – *a certain kind of people.* They can be described as Sound Shapers, the New Tribe, and Risk Takers to name three. There are seven mentioned in this chapter.

Chapter 2 talks about the reformer's mindset. It focuses on who reformers are and how they think. It discusses how the reformer's mindset can change the current narrative over our nations.

Chapter 3 makes the case that every reformer carries a solution. They deal with root causes of problems and provide solutions to deep-seated issues. I share several stories of solution carriers – such as William Wilberforce and the Clapham Group whose persevering actions led to the abolition of slavery and the reform of society plagued by disease, poor educational outcomes and poor nutrition. Fred Swaniker, who through his leadership of the Africa Leadership Group aims to transform Africa by identifying, developing and connecting three million game-changing leaders for Africa by 2060. William Kamkwamba, the boy from Malawi, who at 15 built the first windmill in his village for his parents. He read a book he found in the library after his parents could not pay the school fees to keep him in school. This singular invention caught media attention and he made history as The Boy Who Harnessed the Wind.

I hope these stories inspire you to dig deeper, to want to do more.

Chapters 4 to 7 discuss the four prerequisites required in a reformer that are critical to changing cultures and reforming society. The first is **Character** and Chapter 4 argues that *A Good Character is Non-*

Negotiable. A reformer must be prepared to go on a journey of personal transformation. A journey of transformation that is visible to others – like that of a caterpillar becoming a butterfly.

The second prerequisite is **Competence**. *Chapter 5* starts by defining Competence and it being a convergence of four key qualities. It is also a journey and we discuss the things you can do to embark on the experience of becoming competent. It takes more than passion to change the course of history.

*In **Chapter 6*** we examine **Influence**. Influence shifts cultures. The ability to change what people believe, change how they behave and change how they do things takes a special quality. This chapter attempts to push the boundary and explores the kind of influence that transforms the culture of a sphere, a community or a nation.

Collaboration is the fourth prerequisite. *Chapter 7* states categorically *Reformers Do Not Work Solo – They Collaborate* and warns about the danger of working solo and the initial steps we need to take to enable collaboration. I argue that there are distinct differences between what business schools tell us about collaboration and *true collaboration.* This chapter draws attention to seven simple but important differences. These differences are the fundamental ingredients of *true collaboration.* Not surprisingly there are forces against collaboration we need to contend with – and contend we must. It is these forces that fight against the emergence of new communities of reformers, of an organised army, of a new tribe.

Chapter 8 discusses the building of this new community: What will it take? It will certainly take a significant amount of hard, focused, determined, painful but extremely rewarding work. Radical Love Carriers paying the ultimate price.

The cry in this book is an *empowering cry*. It's a call to pay that price. Arise, Reformer – it is time to form an army and battalions of reform communities. Working together we are stronger.

The nations of Africa can be transformed.

We can do it. Let us do it!

My Dream

I have a dream to see an army of social reformers striding across Africa, the world's second largest continent. An army that understand their assignment and have locked hands together to fulfil that assignment. I can already hear the sound of that army. I hear the stomping of boots. I hear the tanks rolling across the diverse terrain of the 54 nations that make up the continent. Each nation unique with its diversity of cultures, natural minerals and geographical beauty but all struggling with poverty, corruption and unfulfilled potential because of poor educational and health systems.

This army arising is strong and mighty and refuses to do things in the same old way. This army is young and dynamic. They carry an energy. They move with speed, swift as gazelles. They are courageous, not easily frightened or deterred. They are the 'cubs of the Lion of Judah'. They have a roar that you cannot ignore. They stride across the African continent leaving footprints of integrity. Their footprints replace those of corruption, dishonesty and the attitude of 'what's in it for me?' These footprints are not transactional but transformational.

They fight intelligently. They understand their mission and they do not break ranks. They work in unity and unison. They disagree but without destroying that which binds them together. They recognise that they are a formidable force and in their unity they take over territories. They scale walls and defy opposition.

Would you like to join this army?

It is an Army of Reformers. Reformers Arise is a new sound. A new vibration. It can only be heard by those whose ears are tired of hearing the same excuses, tired of complaints. They carry the solutions that will silence the excuses and complaints.

CHAPTER ONE

Reformers –
A Certain Kind of People

There are certain distinguishing qualities of reformers – *the New Tribe* – that mark them and make them stand out. They often defy the status quo and swim against the tide. They are not afraid to stand for truth and have a strong desire for change no matter the cost. They are willing to pay the price.

There are seven distinguishing qualities:

Reformers are Sound Shapers

It is important to understand that every living thing on earth has a sound. The planets each have their own distinct sounds. The trees, the oceans, different species of animals have their recognisable sounds. You know when a dog barks, when a lion roars and a cow moos. These are sounds you hear and you know what to expect to see. Likewise each reformer has his or her own distinct sound that carries the DNA of change. They have a sound you cannot ignore – it carries the sound of their purpose and their life assignment. Within their sound is the power to cause shifts and the power to shape the DNA of cultures. Like a volcano erupting, when a reformer enters the scene, what they release is creatively disruptive. It shakes foundations, traditions and old mindsets. This same disruptive power also has the ability to create something new that affects the lives of others bringing positive change and great impact.

I would like you to be very quiet now. Imagine you are a photographer patiently and quietly observing a herd of gazelles in the Serengeti National Park in Tanzania. You have been there for hours waiting for the herd to arrive, waiting for the perfect shot. Just as you are about to take that shot you hear a loud almost deafening noise. What is the immediate reaction? Out of fear the herd flees; you drop your camera, you miss the moment. The loud noise has caused a scattering.

But sound can also cause a gathering. Again imagine: you are walking down a piazza in the middle of delightful Florence looking for the perfect café to have a much-needed caffeine boost when a sweet melodious sound permeates the atmosphere. It is simply beautiful. You have not heard anything quite like this before. What is your response? You move towards the sound. You want to see who is playing. Others are responding just like you. Everyone attracted by the sound gathers around the musicians, playing with such harmony they cannot be ignored.

The sound of Reformers Arise is a *gathering sound*. It creates a symphony which literally means 'sounding together'. Together they can make things happen that would not ordinarily happen. Together they can redefine circumstances and create history. Reformers as they 'symphonise' can rewrite the life stories of individuals, communities and nations.

Reformers are New Wine in New Wineskin

You spend time preparing new wine. You do not pour it into old wineskin for two reasons: the first is to avoid tainting the taste of the new wine and the second is to avoid the old wineskin bursting and losing your new wine.

Preparing the vineyard, growing your grapes, harvesting and fermenting the grapes to get your new wine is similar to the preparation of social reformers.

You spend time preparing new wine. Social reformers are what the new wine society is waiting for. Each reformer has been shaped, squeezed and moulded to be made fit for purpose. In Chapter 2 we will examine how each one carries a solution, carries a piece of the puzzle. Each one carries a dream in the womb of their spirit. Each one now needs to be trained and equipped to deliver their piece of the puzzle masterfully, efficiently and effectively.

You are first chosen, then prepared, then equipped. Only the good grapes with the right qualities and taste are chosen. A good character, which is non-negotiable, qualifies you to be chosen; your skills and competence prepare you; understanding the mindset of a reformer and your mandate equips you.

Sunday Adelaja declares: *"Where there is no internal transformation, there cannot be external progress and development."*

Reformers are a New Tribe

I am convinced that Africa's transformation lies with the arising of *a new tribe,* a new army of reformers.

The Vice-President of Nigeria, Professor Yemi Osinbajo, in February 2016 said, *"A critical assessment of the list of corrupt persons (in Nigeria) would show that they cut across the tribal, ethnic and religious lines. Such perpetrators and conspirators are in governments, the legislature, the judiciary and the press. They are united, they protect one another, they fight for one another and they are prepared to go down together. They are one tribe and indivisible, regardless of diversity. It is this tribe that confuses the arguments for change in society."*

Professor Osinbajo then added, *"Such a corrupt system can hardly deliver public goods. That system needs to be dismantled if the nation is to progress. We need a **new tribe** of men and women of all faiths, tribes and ethnicities. This will be a tribe of men and women **who are prepared to make the sacrifices and self-constraints** *that are crucial to building a strong society, who are prepared to stick together, fight corruption side by side, and insist on justice even when our friends are at the receiving end."*

As we connect with one another, the new wineskin forms. A new wineskin that embodies the new tribe. A new tribe that shares the same 'language', ethos, culture and vision. A new tribe destined for greatness. Mother Teresa said, *"I can do things you cannot, you can do things I cannot; together we can do great things."*

Reformers are Bridges

I love bridges. I look out for them as I travel the nations because each bridge has a story. I have visited Redding in Northern California four times and each time I have wanted to drive over to the famous Sundial Bridge. I finally got to do this in April 2016 but a surprise was waiting for me. The Sundial Bridge is not a bridge for cars but for pedestrians. There is a lesson here. Bridges have different functions. They transport you across a little stream or a mighty river. They connect communities; they connect one part of a city to another (the famous Golden Gate Bridge in San Francisco or the Third Mainland Bridge in Lagos); they connect nations and even continents (the Bosporus Bridge in Istanbul, Turkey connects Europe and Asia). Bridges facilitate movement. They are enablers. They make things happen.

Reformers are like bridges – they connect people, places and provisions for projects. Without a bridge you are stuck in a particular location. Your movement is hindered. You do not have access to food, goods or provisions.

Reformers as bridges have the ability to connect the present to the future and make that future a reality. They connect people effortlessly. Malcom Gladwell in his book *The Tipping Point: How Little Things Can Make a Big Difference* describes connectors as the *'people in a community who know large numbers of people and who are in the habit of making introductions. A connector is essentially the social equivalent of a computer network hub. They usually know people across an array of social, cultural, professional and economic circles, and make a habit of introducing people who work or live in different circles'*. They are people who *'link us up with the world… people with a special gift for bringing the world together'*. Gladwell attributes the social success of connectors to the fact that *'their ability to span many different worlds is a function of something intrinsic to their personality, a combination of curiosity, self-confidence, sociability and energy'*.

Reformers, as connectors, connect people because they know that some monumental changes require that they come together as change agents and become a 'Change Community'. Without a change community reform is often not sustainable. This brings me to the fifth distinguishing quality.

Reformers Build Change Communities

The ability to collaborate is essential. The willingness to collaborate is critical. A collaborative mindset thinks in a uniquely different way. You understand that each person carries a piece of the puzzle and the puzzle cannot be solved unless all the pieces come together. You also understand that no piece is more important than the other. If a piece is missing the puzzle remains incomplete until that piece is found and added to the puzzle. Each piece is different – it is a well-known fact that no two pieces of the puzzle are the same.

A puzzle actually reminds me of the body. Our body parts are all different. No matter how big or small the part is or how hidden or obvious, each part performs an important function and is almost indispensable. I remember one of the worst flights I ever went on. I crossed the Atlantic ocean from the United Kingdom to the United States of America. I had a bad cold and my nose was completely clogged up. Until that day I had not really paid much attention to my nose but on that flight I could not breathe for over five hours. I thought I would die.

The nasal drops stopped working. I used a hot towel with menthol poured on it given to me by a kind and compassionate air steward. It had no effect. I cried, I prayed, I did all I knew to do and yet no change. My nose was totally blocked. I was breathing through my mouth and I couldn't get off the plane. I was so miserable. At that moment my respect for my nose went up several notches. I laid my hands on my nose and started to honour it. I hailed my nose telling it how wonderful it was and how much I appreciated it and that I was sorry I had not paid it much attention all these years. I must have looked a sight and sounded slightly crazy.

That day I learned that my nose was a very valuable member of my body and without it functioning properly my life was a misery.

This is the same for change makers. If we don't take our rightful position in a Change Community, the lives of many people remain a misery. These people live below their potential because as a piece of the puzzle you have not moved into position and taken your place. Change Communities are most effective when the members of that community exhibit certain qualities and live a distinct lifestyle. We will talk more about this in Chapter 4 – *A Good Character is Non-Negotiable*.

Reformers are Risk Takers

Reformers know how to walk on water. They know how to step out into the great unknown not knowing what lies in front of them. You walk on water when you leave your comfortable lifestyle and go across the world to a land whose socioeconomic indicators classify it as an emerging nation or a developing country, not knowing what lies in store for you. The story of Heidi Baker is one of a woman who has laid down her life for the love of a nation – the nation of Mozambique. Heidi Baker, often described as a modern day Mother Teresa, grew up in Southern California and moved to Mozambique with her husband, Rolland, in 1995 after her PhD programme at King's College, London. They set up Iris Global, and with minimal resources they have over the last 20 years changed whole communities. They started with one orphanage – one formerly owned by the government – and today Iris Global's operations have expanded to include free health clinics, well-drilling, village feeding programmes, the operation of primary and secondary schools, and cottage industries. They have walked on water and not drowned.

Like some people, I have had to walk on water several times. The Education Hub, a state of the art equipping and training centre with the Imaginal Centre, Innovation Centre, the iCafé and the Dream Centre became a reality as I walked on water. I had only N30 (less than $1) as I started a journey that required N24million (approximately $160,000).

The journey started in March 2013. I had moved from Abuja, the capital of Nigeria, back to Lagos. The move was unexpected and unanticipated but that is another story. I arrived back in Lagos in August 2012 and my dear friend whom I fondly call Sunshine offered me her office to work from. I needed somewhere to go to on a daily basis to stay productive. After six comfortable months, just as I was settling in, Sunshine called me one day while I was on a Learning Journey to Canada and with great excitement said, "Reformer, Reformer, I think I have seen your office." Was I looking for an office? I didn't know I was looking for an office! I was happy where I was – camping in her office.

She said a company was moving out of the first floor of her building and she felt it would be a wonderful place for us. I asked her about the size of the office and when she told me I almost passed out. It was roughly three times the size of her office, which not only had office space for her and her staff, but also a conference room and a training room. I screamed. Where would I get the money for such a huge space? Who needed that kind of space – certainly not me? I had only two full-time and one part-time staff. Incubator Africa had just opened its door for business. Where would I get N10million ($66,000) for rent and service charge for one year? Where would I get the resources for renovation and office set-up, which I later found out required another N14million ($90,000)?

As I laughed I heard a small still voice say, "This is for the Education Hub." You guessed right – the next question I asked was, "What is the Education Hub?" Over the next few months as I said yes and took the risk of fulfilling a dream I had carried for over 20 years and walked on water, I watched the money flow in from unusual sources. I had no idea that the dream would materialise in this manner.

The first N12million ($80,000) came as I did something most unusual. I was invited to speak at a forum that looked after the poor and needy. As I spoke that day I found myself sharing the dream of the Education Hub. I mentioned I needed a lot of money (I was careful not to mention the amount) and that all I had was N30. Then I asked a question: How many of them knew that the money I needed would come in because I believe? Everyone shouted in agreement.

As I left the forum a young man approached me who said he felt very strongly he and another lady (the organiser of the forum) were to give me N12,000 ($80). Tears came to my eyes as he placed 12 notes each of N1,000 into my hands. I was N12,000 richer but a far cry from the N10million I needed to take possession of the place. I thanked him as I gently wept and got into my car.

The next morning as I woke up I heard the same gentle voice that said, "This is for the Education Hub" clearly say, "Lay the 12 notes on the floor." I obeyed: I laid the 12 notes in two lines, each line had six notes each. This may sound crazy but wait for it! I was to now speak over each note and as I spoke I was to mentally convert each N1,000 note into N1,000,000. Yes, you read correctly – one million! I had nothing to lose so I did what I was told.

Within the next two weeks I received N8million and in another month a corporate donor gave us another N10million. As I followed divine instructions it unlocked hidden riches in unusual places. Don't ask me how it works. But I know not being afraid to walk on water, to keep stepping forward into the unknown, triggers the supernatural.

Reformers are History Makers

'I have a Dream' – **Martin Luther King Jr**

'Never, Never, Never, Never Give Up'
– **Winston Churchill**

These are not mere words. They carry a power and a sound that reverberates through history. The sound of freedom and justice. The sound these men released opened up a window, a portal in time, that allowed certain significant life-changing actions to take place. These words birthed a nation. We know the history makers who said them. These were individuals who rose and stood for a cause. Their words caused a movement to arise and cultures to be shifted.

They were angry, they were passionate, they were resolute and refused to give up. You are angry, you are passionate and now you need to arise, be resolute and refuse to give up. You are a history maker. I have a definition of history makers that I love: *if you don't do what you were created to do it will not get done.* You have a dream, you have a cause. If you don't pursue your dream or your cause it may never get done. You will live and the world will never know you passed through it.

Martin Luther King Jr before he died said, *"If you haven't found something for which you're willing to die, you're not fit to live."* In the famous speech he made the day before he was killed, King said, *"I've been to the mountaintop"*... and *"When people get caught up with that which is right and they are willing to sacrifice for it, there is no stopping point short of victory. But it takes a willingness to develop a kind of dangerous unselfishness."*

You can be a history maker on a global level, within a nation, a community, an organisation or a village. It is what you do that counts. There are lives that are significantly impacted because you arose and took action. You were willing and you were resolute and you didn't give up.

The story of William Kamkwamba is a fascinating one. I first heard of him when he became a student in the inaugural class of the African Leadership Academy, an amazing school set up in South Africa to raise a new generation of African leaders. In 2013, *Time Magazine* named William one of the '30 People Under 30 Changing the World'.

William was born in a family of relative poverty and relied primarily on farming to survive. According to his biography, *The Boy Who Harnessed the Wind*, his father had been a rough fighting man who changed after becoming a Christian. A crippling famine forced Kamkwamba to drop out of school, and he was not able to return because his family could not afford the tuition fees. In a desperate attempt to retain his education, Kamkwamba began to visit the school library frequently. It was there he discovered his love for electronics.

Kamkwamba, after reading a book called *Using Energy*, decided to create a makeshift windmill. He built a windmill to power a few electrical appliances in his family's home using blue gum trees, bicycle parts and materials collected in a local scrapyard. This singular invention caught media attention and he made history as 'The Boy Who Harnessed the Wind'. He was invited to speak at TEDGlobal 2007 in Arusha, Tanzania. His speech moved the audience and several venture capitalists pledged to help finance his secondary school education. Today he is a graduate of Dartmouth College based in New Hampshire, USA.

He has built a solar-powered water pump that supplied the first drinking water in his village and two other windmills. Kamkwamba is the subject of the documentary film *William and the Windmill*, which won the Grand Jury Prize for Best Documentary Feature at the 2013 South by Southwest Film Festival in Austin, Texas.

William Kamkwamba is a History Maker.

CHAPTER TWO

The Reformer's Mindset

In the last chapter I spent some time highlighting what reformers are like. I used words like sound shapers, bridges and history makers. In this section I would like to focus a little more on *who* they are and their mindset. If I was woken suddenly from sleep and asked to summarise in a few words who reformers are, I would say they are Radical Love Carriers. I believe it is this singular quality that motivates their heart of sacrifice, drives their ability to defer gain and propels their burning vision and unrelenting passion to transform a life, an organisation or a nation. This makes a reformer *Undaunted* and *Unstoppable*. These two words are the titles of two bestsellers by Christine Caine, co-founder of the A21 Campaign, an organisation dedicated to addressing the injustice of human trafficking in the 21st century.

Undaunted by discouragement, disappointments or difficulties, reformers are to keep running their race towards destiny. *Unstoppable* by obstacles, wrong turns and unexpected circumstances, they keep moving forward undeterred. Radical love for anything makes you unstoppable. You cannot think of anything else. Your life is consumed by it. Your purpose is defined by it. You live it, you breathe it. You are willing to do anything for the object of your love. That love births two incredible qualities: passion and sacrifice. A wise proverb says: 'Love is as strong as death'. Love is powerful and radical love even more so.

It was this radical love that gave Martin Luther King Jr the strength to offer himself as a living sacrifice and pay the price for the emergence of President Barack Obama several decades later.

It was this same radical love that made it possible for me to visit post-apartheid South Africa in January 2013 as a solo traveller, proudly African with no fear of going anywhere in that country at any time (within reason of course). Nelson Mandela had paid the price. He served in prison for 25 years. It was my visit to Robben Island that truly opened my eyes to the price paid. There were many others like Nelson Mandela who served prison time and some served more years than he did. I saw the cells of men who had been incarcerated for more than 30 years. This was not a comfortable prison by any means. The tiny room could only contain a single bed. The prisoners were forced to cut stones daily – 12-14 hours every day, every week, every month, year after year. I left Robben Island sober and yet with a sense of victory. These men were unstoppable.

And so must you be. You cannot afford to compromise your purpose for a 'morsel of bread'. Remember the Bible story of the twins Esau and Jacob? Remember how Esau the older twin lost his birthright for a morsel of porridge because he could not wait, because he could not defer gain? An Esau mindset is unable to pay the price for a better tomorrow, unable to defer gain and stand until the challenges blow over. An Esau mindset is dangerous and has aborted many destinies and caused many others to be shipwrecked.

Your passion and your vision should burn so strong that it sustains the seasons of constraint and imprisonment that you will experience. The vision of a post-apartheid South Africa sustained Nelson Mandela. The vision of a casteless India sustained Mahatma Gandhi. The vision of freed black men and women where they would be judged by the content of their character and not the colour of their skin sustained Martin Luther King Jr.

Their vision spoke to the high price they would have to pay to see the end of what angered them the most. As reformers you are addressing deep-seated issues. Monumental problems that cannot often be dealt with by wishing them away. Radical love, sacrificial service and unrelenting passion will hold on until the very end, until the vision is realised.

The Reformer's Mindset

The British Dictionary defines mindset as *'the ideas and attitudes with which a person approaches a situation, especially when these are seen as being difficult to alter'*.

The Cambridge Dictionary defines it as *'a person's way of thinking and their opinions'*.

The Reformer's Mindset can Change the Narrative

The mindset that has governed and ruled the nations of Africa has been one of greed and corruption, of chaos and disorder, of injustice and poverty. This mindset embraces status quo and has kept many African nations in the throes of poverty. Though some may argue that there has been significant progress in many nations, I believe that these are still only spotlights in the midst of darkness. They are only oases of development in the vast desert of underdevelopment. It is time to change this narrative. The reformer's mindset is wired to change this narrative. It is unique, different and has the ability to rewrite the stories of the continent.

It has a Love for Country that is Palpable

The reformer's mindset has a love for country that is palpable. Self is dead. They are often chided for being too patriotic and advised to slow down as they cannot fix everything. They are not consultants who are hired to provide solutions. Reformers are motivated by a deeper measure of zeal – *an intense passionate desire*

– that makes them offer their services, gifts and talents even if there is no financial reward. A multinational consultant will not work without financial gain. I respect that. It is important you get paid. But what I want us to see is the mindset of a reformer and what motivates him or her. They are motivated by sacrificial love and a servant heart.

It is a Flame of Fire

The mindset of a reformer is like a flame of fire. It starts with a passionate, burning desire that won't leave you and then becomes a fire that consumes you. As you meet other 'flames of fire', something begins to happen inside of you. Your thinking, your motivation and your actions begin to change. You are no longer comfortable with the status quo. You are tired of what is wrong and totally fed up with feeling helpless and doing nothing.

Reformers, therefore, derive joy from reforming and re-ordering structures that are chaotic, disorderly and out of alignment. The reformer brings them into order. They see injustice and are compelled to bring justice; they see wrongdoing and have no rest until they bring correction. They are wired to restructure, reorganise and re-order.

It is a Creative Mindset

To reform you have to be able to create what is new. This is a design mindset, an imaginative mindset able to create the new through diverse expressive mediums. Through words, pictures and other creative expressions, the reformer captures the new structure and proceeds to assemble with other builders what it is they have seen.

It is a Collaborative Mindset

The reformer's mindset is willing to collaborate and to work with others as a team. Recently I read the following on a social media post that perhaps tells us that more people are understanding the need to work together: *This is our country but to move forward we need to work as a team. This means uplifting one another, focusing on helping each other. A team cannot win if everyone goes their own way. We only win as a nation if we work together.*

Reformers are arising and taking their positions. They are working together to build a new tribe, a new community with a new mindset. Chapters 7 and 8 speak specifically on Collaboration and Building Communities.

It is a Transformational and Not Transactional Mindset

Reformers are not motivated by short-term gains. They are in it for the long haul. They are not transactional but transformational in action and in outlook. They are willing to walk away from activities that might benefit them but harm the public good. They are not afraid to do what is right, neither are they shy to be counted among the new tribe. In fact, that is their new identity and they breathe and feed off it. It is an identity that can be scary and unappealing. But reformers are not moved by outward appearances. Remaining true to their values and character is what distinguishes them.

It is a Fighter's Mindset

Think of a fighter – a professional boxer or a trained soldier. They use their energy, power and prowess to engage in a physical activity that results in one person winning the fight. A reformer's mindset brings the same energy, power and prowess to the 'reform arena'. They fight for a cause – to right wrongs and injustices. They fight, not giving up until they see change.

Reformers are warriors fighting for the new identity of their nation. They do not look like regular soldiers. Instead they wear the identities of their assignment – the innovative teacher, journalist, politician, government official, actor, business person. They fight in their spheres to bring order and development.

It is a Strategic Mindset

The reformer's mindset effortlessly understands the fundamentals of strategic thinking, knowing the *What, When, Where,* with *Whom* and *How.* One of my mentors often warned that many people find it hard to answer the *How* question. This is often where people struggle to execute on dreams and plans. Answering the *How* question in a practical and detailed manner is a talent you can grow and strengthen.

How do you do this? There are several ways to do this, but let us highlight a few:

1. Learn to ask the right questions. Learn to look beyond the surface and dig deeper.

2. Engage in the art of deep, reflective thinking.

3. Don't always take the easy route or the path of least resistance. Learn to walk down the paths less travelled and confront issues if need be.

The art of thinking deeply is not easy as it requires time and space which everyday life competes with. You have to consciously and intentionally set aside a period of time needed to receive and think. Something I learned to do a few years ago was to shut down for a day or two and just think. I would think through processes, actions that need to be taken and answer questions as they arose in my mind. Then I would write down these answers in a journal (always keep a journal as your memory will fail you). Finally, I would bounce the answers off a few individuals that I called 'counsellors' to ensure that I was seeing the full picture and not missing anything. There is power in getting feedback that strengthens your ability to be more strategic in your thinking.

The Reformer's Mindset is Values Driven

The reformer's mindset is rooted in core values that guide decision making and shape the work they do. Core values such as Integrity, Truth, Selflessness, and Loyalty are their guiding principles, the compass that leads them and the anchors that keep them steady. In Chapter 4 where we discuss *A Good Character is Non-Negotiable* we deal with some of these values in detail.

> *The reformer's mindset is undeniable.*
> *It is different, you cannot ignore it.*

CHAPTER THREE

Reformers Deal with Root Causes and Provide Solutions to Deep-Seated Issues

I remember waking up one morning a few years ago with a cry of frustration erupting from my heart. I remember expressing my frustration and anger in words. I had served three Ministers of Education in five years and nothing was changing. In fact the problems in education in many states of the country I was living in at the time seemed to be getting worse. The indicators were gloomy and depressing. I declared with a loud voice to anyone who would care to listen, *"I am tired of half-hearted, weak and mundane attempts by governments to address problems of monumental proportions. I am tired of budgets that have little impact and where the already inadequate approved budgets are not executed. Our educational systems will not change unless we take some difficult decisions. Foundations need to be reconstructed. Structural, functional and systemic change is required. We have to stop pretending that we are taking action and with all sincerity and conviction execute the far-reaching decisions that need to be taken."*

Every Reformer Carries a Solution

The 'far-reaching decisions' that need to be taken are the solutions reformers carry. Reformers are wired to deal with root causes of monumental problems that nations face. They don't deal with the superficial, the mundane that can easily be solved without sleepless nights and sacrifice. This is why reformers are not just consultants, though they may deliver solutions using the consulting approach. They carry the piece of a puzzle that solves a problem that will impact lives today and tomorrow and for generations to come. In order to correctly deliver these solutions there are four prerequisites to changing cultures and reforming societies namely Character, Competence, Influence and Collaboration that reformers need to understand and embrace. Let me give some examples.

William Wilberforce carried the solution to the end of slavery and the reform of moral values for 19th century England. He did not work alone but was part of a group – the famous Clapham Group (which I will discuss in greater detail in both Chapters 7 and 8 on Collaboration and Building Communities respectively).

William Wilberforce used the four prerequisites (Character, Competence, Influence and Collaboration) to transform 19th century England. His character as a Radical Love Carrier paid a price for 18 years; he deferred gain, and driven by passion and vision, he used his influence in Parliament as a law-giver to prevail until he saw the change he fought for on his dying bed.

Drawing from the work done by the British Broadcasting Corporation (BBC), let us further examine how the life of William Wilberforce creates a *convergence* of the four qualities that make an effective reformer.

William Wilberforce was born on 24 August 1759 in Hull, the son of a wealthy merchant. He studied at Cambridge University where he began a lasting friendship with a future prime minister, William Pitt the Younger. In 1780, Wilberforce became Member of Parliament for Hull, later representing Yorkshire. His dissolute lifestyle changed completely when he became an evangelical Christian, and in 1790 he joined a leading group known as the Clapham Sect. This change in his mindset prompted him to become interested in social reform, particularly the improvement of factory conditions in Britain. Also the abolitionist Thomas Clarkson had an enormous influence on Wilberforce. He and others were campaigning for an end to the slave trade. Wilberforce was persuaded to lobby for the abolition of the slave trade and for 18 years he regularly introduced anti-slavery motions in Parliament. The campaign was supported by many members of the Clapham Sect and other abolitionists who raised public awareness of their cause with pamphlets, books, rallies and petitions.

In 1807, the slave trade was finally abolished, but this did not free those who were already slaves. It was not until 1833 that an Act was passed giving freedom to all slaves in the British Empire. Wilberforce died on 29 July 1833, a few days after the Act was passed. He lived to see the change that he fought and died for.

This truly is a powerful convergence of Character, Competence, Influence, Collaboration and Community. Wilberforce was trained (Cambridge University – Competence). He recognised other reformers and connected with them (Collaboration). He experienced personal transformation (Character) that equipped him to stand resolute and determined to reform a system that cost him his entire life. He understood his purpose, accepted the assignment and collaborated with those that would facilitate the achievement of the assignment. He had a special advantage (lasting friendship with the prime minister); he ran for office and became a Member of Parliament (political influence). He used this influence and the power released through collaborative effort to do the seemingly impossible – the execution of deep-seated societal reform from the roots.

Let's bring it home to the 21st century. Africa has a failing educational system that needs a total overhaul. This cannot be done by a few individuals carrying a consulting mindset. It will take an army of solution carriers trained in their respective spheres of education, from early childhood to secondary school education and tertiary education, working together to deliver profound solutions in areas such as teacher education. It will take solution carriers that can and must redesign our curriculum to deliver the quality and type of students that the African continent needs to take it from Third World to First World. Students that recognise the cultural uniqueness and nuances of the continent. Students that are Radical Love Carriers and are ready to take responsibility for addressing deep-seated issues. We need to birth a new DNA in the African child. Create new images that will bring forth transformed societies.

This will not happen by pursuing business as usual. And this is why there is a growing excitement about new initiatives like the African Leadership Academy (ALA) in Johannesburg, South Africa. ALA is a unique educational institution established to raise the African leaders of tomorrow. It is an intensive two-year academic programme that combines the Cambridge University A-Level curriculum with three other core elements: Leadership Education, African Studies with an emphasis on African history and the cultural understanding of Africa, and finally a well-developed entrepreneurship component (remember William Kamkwamba, *The Boy Who Harnessed the Wind*, highlighted in Chapter 1 – he attended ALA*)*.

ALA is an interesting institution birthed as a dream first conceived in the heart of a young man, Fred Swaniker, who is deeply passionate about Africa and believes that the missing ingredient on the continent is good leadership. I first met Fred when he came to Nigeria to interview the pioneer class for ALA. We were paired together as interview partners. His passion was infectious. He was polite, gentle and extremely focused. You could feel his 'can-do' energy and unstoppable posture. Little did I know that this was the beginning of greatness. Today he is the founder of the African Leadership 'Group' – an ecosystem of organisations that includes African Leadership Academy (ALA), African Leadership Network, Africa Advisory Group and Africa Leadership University (ALU) that took off with its inaugural class of 180 in October 2015. ALU intends to resist the pressure to conduct tertiary education the way it has always been done. It will challenge existing beliefs so that they only *'keep what works, and reimagine the rest'.* ALU's mission is to *'create a more prosperous and peaceful Africa by developing the next generation of ethical and entrepreneurial African Leaders'.* Collectively, the institutions under the African Leadership Group aim to transform Africa by identifying, developing and connecting three million game-changing leaders for Africa by 2060.

Fred Swaniker is a strong nexus, another example of a powerful convergence of Character, Competence,

Calling Out a People of Dignity to Influence and Action

Influence, Collaboration and Community. He has an MBA from Stanford Business School where he was named an Arjay Miller Scholar, a distinction awarded to the top 10% of each graduating class. He has been recognised as a Young Global Leader by the World Economic Forum, by *Forbes Magazine* as one of the top 10 young 'power men' in Africa, and by Echoing Green as one of the 15 best emerging social entrepreneurs in the world. Fred began his professional career as a consultant with McKinsey & Company, and it was while working there that he spotted a significant gap in the preparation and education of African children prior to their going to university. He did not work alone. He teamed up with other passionate competent reformers to establish the dream – ALA. Without fellow co-founders Chris Bradford, Acha Leke and Peter Mombaur there would be no ALA as we know it today.

Chris Bradford, a graduate of Yale and Stanford University, was a former consultant with Boston Consulting Group. It was at Stanford that Fred and Chris began to build ALA. At Stanford Chris was named a Siebel Scholar, a distinction given to five students for academic excellence and extracurricular leadership. Like Fred he also received an Echoing Green Fellowship as one of the 'leading emerging entrepreneurs in the world'.

Acha Leke, co-founder of ALA, is an influential partner in McKinsey & Company, a leading global consulting firm. In 2008 he was selected as Young Global Leader by the World Economic Forum and Africa's Young Investment Professional of the Year at the Alternative Investment Awards.

Peter Mombaur, also a co-founder, met Fred and Acha while at McKinsey & Company at the Johannesburg office. Today he is the Managing Director of Tana Africa Capital.

Together these four men as highly competent individuals, through collaboration and influence, have created an educational institution ecosystem that cannot be ignored.

Otto Orandaam did not go to Yale nor was he at Stanford. He did not go to any of the top global schools. He went to the University of Port Harcourt in Nigeria. Otto started his journey in his twenties with an anger, a love and a deep concern for the children he saw every day playing under a bridge on his way to his first job. He was working in a bank serving as a National Youth Service Corp member (NYSC) after completing his first degree. The NYSC is a one-year programme that every graduate in Nigeria is expected to complete. It was set up by the Nigerian government to involve the country's graduates in the development of the country. It started with extremely lofty ideals, which it has unfortunately not lived up to in recent years.

During his National Youth Service, week after week Otto saw these young children playing in muddy dirty water at a time when they should be going to school. There were thousands of others who saw these children doing the wrong thing at the wrong time including myself. But only one person responded – Otto Orandaam.

He became consumed by this picture. He saw young lives being wasted. It represented unfulfilled potential. One day he couldn't take it anymore. He arranged with a few friends to visit this fishing community in the middle of Lagos, the former capital of Nigeria, one of the largest megacities in the world – 15 million people and counting. He spent the whole day there observing and asking questions.

Today Slum2School is a major initiative addressing the problem of 'out-of-school' children. It is an intervention to advocate for and improve access and quality of education for disadvantaged children in slums and remote communities. It started as a concern for injustice and unrealised potential, a dream to help one child, and now hundreds of children are placed in schools. There is now a volunteer force of over 3,000 young people from over 25 countries working alongside Otto. They mentor these children, they provide much-needed learning materials and work with the parents and the community to give support. They have led campaigns to renovate dilapidated schools in remote communities and equip slum schools with more facilities like computer rooms, libraries and health centres.

We see yet again a powerful convergence of Character, Competence, Influence, Collaboration and community.

Otto's passion and commitment to change has received recognition. He started small; he started with the problem he encountered on a daily basis and took a decision to do something about it. He stepped out. He attracted and gathered like-minded young reformers. Otto's 'sound' is compelling and he draws you in with his genuine kindness and commitment to fight for the children who live in the slums of our cities. Otto is determined to ensure that their future is not defined by where life placed them.

He is now a recipient of several awards, starting with the Lagos State Honours Award, as the most outstanding corps member in 2012; the Future Awards for Innovation in Education in 2012 and 2013; and was recognised by the Presidency as one of the top 100 Nigerian youths.

All these reformers demonstrate that the dreams we carry in the womb of our spirit are very often the profound solutions society needs. Those dreams can be ignited by passion for something that may or may not yet exist or anger at the existence of a problem or situation. These solutions executed by reformers attack the problem at its roots, at the foundation. It is therefore not about applying a band-aid or a plaster to deep wounds.

It is Not About Band-Aids

I have worked with several public sector organisations and agencies, and I am slowly and painfully realising that many of their actions are veiled half-hearted attempts at dealing with deep-seated issues with band-aids, otherwise known as plasters, in most African countries. Unfortunately, band-aids do not stop bleeding, they do not bring healing. Yet we are consistently using band-aids to cover societal wounds that need major surgery. Wounds that need debridement to heal, wounds that need the 'gunk' to first be evacuated. Some of these wounds are so grievous you need to amputate the affected limb so that other parts of the body do not become infected and the patient dies.

The application of band-aids where surgery is required often leads to death. Look at our societies and you see dead institutions and dead projects strewn across the landscape of the economy. It is time to go beyond band-aids, beyond the application of plasters.

Paul Collier in his book *The Bottom Billion: Why the Poorest Countries are Failing and What Can Be Done About It* criticised politicians of these failing states for using the bottom billion merely for photo opportunities, rather than promoting real transformation. They don't go beyond the surface, proffering superficial solutions that do not address the fundamental issues.

This is why the definition of the word *Reform* that appeals to me emphasises the word broken up into its two definitive components – *Re-form*. To re-form a thing speaks to structural changes; to the reconstruction of the outward appearance of a thing so that what exists after the process of reformation is so significant that it often does not resemble its original state. I support the school of thought that believes reformation of foundations, structures and systems must precede the transformation of a society if it is to be successful, effective and sustainable. Let us examine two key examples of 're-form'. The first example is where the foundations of a society were re-formed and re-defined. One of the best examples of this is the Singapore Story described in the book *From Third World to First World: The Singapore Story: 1965-2000* by Lee Kuan Yew. The second example of re-form is the change of philosophy, structures and processes that took place in Finland that transformed the educational system now described as one of the best in the world.

These two examples show how well-articulated reform initiatives implemented over a considerable period of time transform a nation in the case of Singapore, and a sector in the case of Finland. The results, which we will see in the stories below, were not overnight successes. It has taken several decades (30 years and more) of executing the right solutions to change the trajectory of development in these two nations. In Singapore the visionary outlook and reform mindset of Lee Kuan Yew, the prime minister for 30 years, played a critical role in creating the ecosystem that laid the foundation for Singapore's outstanding economic growth. In Finland the story is that of a collective group of people – the teachers and policymakers – who developed educational policies that shaped the character, intellect and thinking of students. Teachers in Finland are proudly called the 'candles of society'.

Laying New Foundations: From Third World to First: The Singapore Story 1965-2000

Lee Kuan Yew (1933-2015), fondly known as the father of modern-day Singapore, laid a new foundation for the Singapore of today.

Today Singapore, a former British Colonial trading post, once described as a 'colonial backwater' is now transformed into an economic powerhouse and is a thriving Asian metropolis, with an airline consistently listed in the top three airlines in the world, one of the best airports, one of the busiest ports of trade, and the world's fourth highest per capita real income. When Lee Kuan Yew became prime minister in 1959, Singapore had a per capita GDP of $400. When he left office in 1999 it had risen dramatically to $12,000, and by the year 2000 when *The Singapore Story* was written it was $22,000. In 2015 Singapore's GDP was $56,000.

I remember my first visit to Singapore in the late 1990s. I was impressed by the magnificent roads; the stunning high-rise apartments – a symbol of their successful public housing reform; their sprawling five-star malls and their beautiful parks. I found it hard to believe that this was once a 'colonial backwater' with goats and chickens running around on the same highway that connected the airport to the city. Lee Kuan Yew and his team laid a new foundation for governance, service excellence and economic prowess.

They transformed the public service, established industrial parks, changed laws, redefined the educational and health systems and raised a new generation of Singaporeans that could compete on the global platform with enviable competence and great work ethics. Lee Kuan Yew challenged the status quo.

On the day Lee Kuan Yew and his cabinet were being sworn in they all wore white to symbolise that integrity and doing the right thing would be their watchword. The foundation that was laid then has now made Singapore the most ethical and business-friendly environment in Asia. Business executives see Singapore as Asia's least bureaucratic place in which to operate, with one of the best banking and financial systems in the region and the world.

The Secrets of the Finnish Educational System

An Education Reform Team consisting of eight members went on a Learning Journey to Finland in early 2012. We embarked on this journey because the Finnish educational system works. It did not always work and it did not achieve this status overnight. Thirty years ago the Finns decided to embark on a journey to reform their education sector with the child at the centre of their vision; they committed to changing whatever was needed (from laws, policies, methods to infrastructure) and now Finland has become the Jerusalem to which the world flocks in order to glean from their remarkable success story! There are certain key words that describe the educational system in Finland: equity, quality, efficiency, and no dead ends. The educational system gives equal opportunity to every child and adult to develop their potential and become all they are destined to be.

The word equity rings through the education plans for most countries – it's at the centre for the United Nations global campaign Education for All but it is in Finland that we saw the true implementation of this vision and aspiration. Every child that lives in Finland, regardless of place of birth (urban or rural), of social status, of race or creed, has undenied and unfettered access to quality education. This for us was a key takeaway – the implementation of education as a basic human right for all. A person is educated in his/her own time, according to his/her own self-development. A child has the right to learn in the way that he/she can best learn in a qualitative environment. And we realised that it is this exceptional quality education that continuously puts Finland ahead of many nations in the global economy. It has made Finland number one in international comparisons (Programme for International Student Assessment – PISA 2000 and 2009).

Let's review a few of the steps that Finland took. First they revolutionised teacher education. This has eliminated the need for school inspectors, a major arm of most national school systems.

Pasi Sahlberg explains that although Finland has built world-class teacher education programmes and teachers are reasonably well paid, the true difference *"is that teachers in Finland may exercise their professional knowledge and judgment both widely and freely in their schools. They control curriculum, student assessment, school improvement, and community involvement."* Many are drawn to the profession by its *"compelling societal mission and its condition of autonomy and support"* (Sahlberg, P (2011) *Finnish Lessons: What can the world learn from educational change in Finland?*).

Consequently there is an undeniable desire and passion for well-qualified, intelligent people to become teachers rather than doctors or lawyers. The competition for places is stiff, with higher education institutions like Jyvaskyla University receiving over 2,800 applications for 80 places. We saw clear evidence of the professionalism and passion of the teachers; the excellent content of the curriculum; the unique delivery of guidance and counselling in schools; the excellent management of schools by school leadership; and the joy in the classroom of the children who thrive in a child-centred environment. This is not teaching in the 19th and 20th century – this is learning. At the centre is the child, the young adult, the matured adult – the learner. We saw this at the primary schools and vocational schools we visited.

A second major step was the 'professionalisation' of every career path and the emphasis on lifelong learning. We learned that every vocation and career has become a profession, from the cook in a restaurant to the professor in a university. Every job has an education path. This speaks to close collaboration between the job market and the education system, which is also a reflection of the collaborative nature of the system.

The Finnish educational system works. It works because government has made education its priority; government has devolved power to the municipals, schools, teachers and students. What we saw was an extraordinary and innovative educational system.

I could go on but the message is clear: deep-seated problems in our nations require deep-rooted re-forms. These reforms are executed by individuals of character, competence and influence. Individuals who know that to achieve purpose they have to learn how to collaborate with others.

CHAPTER FOUR

A Good Character is Non-Negotiable

"Over the years I have seen that if character issues are compromised, it hurts the whole team and eventually undermines the mission."

Bill Hybels – *Courageous Leadership*

This chapter seeks to define a standard of character that is required for change in Africa to happen. It is a standard that is non-negotiable. This is not about paying lip service to character traits such as integrity, honesty, loyalty and excellence. This is about becoming a people that will doggedly apply the right traits and values that transform a nation.

This chapter is not about good character for the sake of good character. Unless, as Africans, we exhibit a certain standard of non-negotiable character traits we will not become a First World continent. It will not happen. Before going any further it is important you understand the point I am trying to make here. I can already feel the tension and even fear of not being able to meet this invisible mark of excellence. Please hear me: the Gold Standard of Non-negotiable Character Traits is not a legalistic approach to character formation. It is not a list of dos and don'ts. It is not about a daily struggle to be good enough. It is not about a lifetime of missing the mark and being miserable because you failed.

This Gold Standard of Non-negotiable Character Traits is an outcome of a process. It is who you are when no one is watching. Do you walk in integrity; do you uphold what is true and just; do you do what is convenient; do you sacrifice truth on the altar of compromise?

Who you are in the dark when no one is watching and who you are when people *are* watching become one and the same. There is no discrepancy. Glitches and wrinkles are ironed out as you *become*. This journey is important as *personal transformation precedes national transformation*. You really cannot be a change maker, a reformer, without a visible journey of personal transformation. It should be visible to you and visible to others. Your journey of transformation could be likened to that of a caterpillar becoming a butterfly. Like the caterpillar you leave your old ways and embrace the new creation – *the butterfly*.

Why is this important? Without question, good leadership at every level is critical to Africa's transformation whether it is at the legislative, judiciary or executive level of government. It is important if you want to see educational and health systems work effectively and efficiently. Good leadership is critical for the success of large and small organisations. It is what differentiates strong and successful nations from failing states.

Remember I mentioned at the beginning of this book, in the Preface, that I asked some young reformers a series of questions that focused on what they thought were the main obstacles to Nigeria's progress to becoming a Second World nation. Their answers without exception pointed to corruption, poor leadership, unethical behaviour and lack of unity as the bane of African societies. In a quest to redefine a different future, Dr Mo Ibrahim established a foundation that celebrates good leadership. Mo Ibrahim is a wealthy Sudanese philanthropist and businessman who founded the telecommunication company Celtel International in 1998, sold it for $3.4 billion in 2005 and established the Mo Ibrahim Foundation in 2006. I first met Mo Ibrahim in 2003 when I served as a member of the International Alumni Board of the London Business School and he served on the Africa Advisory Board.

The Foundation started off by identifying that two of the greatest issues Africa contends with are leadership and governance. The foundation therefore set out to bring meaningful change to the continent of Africa by celebrating excellence in leadership and providing tools to support progress in governance. In 2007 the Ibrahim Prize for Excellence and Achievement in African Leadership was established. It is awarded to a former Executive Head of State or Government by an independent prize committee composed of eminent individuals including two Nobel Peace Prize Laureates.

The prize is an initial payment of $5 million plus $200,000 a year for life. This is the world's largest prize, exceeding the $1.3 million Nobel Peace Prize. The standard required to win this award is high. Though meant to be an annual award, the last award was in 2014 as in 2015 no one was found worthy to receive the award. This is the fifth time the award has failed to find a suitable winner in its 10 years of existence. There were no winners in 2009, 2010, 2012 and 2013. The Mo Ibrahim prize has clearly become a valuable benchmark for excellence on the continent. Dr Ibrahim said, *"When we launched the prize 10 years ago, we deliberately set a very high bar. We want the prize to shine a spotlight on outstanding leadership to provide role models right across society."*

This is the new standard for Africa. Until we uphold a culture of good character and insist that the attributes of integrity, honesty and hard work are non-negotiable, we will continue to struggle as a continent. It is time to develop a new identity and to fight to infuse these qualities into the DNA of our nation's genetic pool.

A New Identity: the Lifestyle that Differentiates

By now you will have noticed that I refer to the Gold Standard of Non-negotiable Character Traits. These are traits that I find are sadly missing in the nations that are at the bottom of the Transparency Index compiled by a respected global organisation, Transparency International. There are three character attributes I would like to focus on that can be considered as non-negotiable. They can be thought of as three legs of a tripod: without one the other two cannot stand:

- Unflinching Integrity
- Undiluted Honesty
- Undeniable Hard Work

Unflinching Integrity and Undiluted Honesty

The word integrity comes from the Latin *integer* meaning 'whole'. Nicky Gumbel, the visionary of the Alpha course that has won global acclaim, describes integrity as *"an undivided life, a 'wholeness' that comes from qualities such as honesty and consistency of character. It means we act according to the values, beliefs and principles we claim to hold."*

The Former US President Dwight D. Eisenhower, Supreme Commander of the Allied Forces in Western Europe during World War II, more pointedly said, *"The supreme quality for leadership is unquestionably integrity. Without it, no real success is possible, no matter whether it is . . . on a football field, in an army, or in an office."*

Integrity is not convenient. It is not easy. It can be painful and difficult. Sometimes it is just easier to play ball. But as a reformer that intends to be part of this new army you cannot play ball. Be prepared to walk down the road less travelled.

Closely tied to this is **undiluted honesty.** No white lies. No half-truths. No embellishments. It is nothing but the truth no matter the cost. We have to become a people who are willing to 'fall on their swords'. It is time for the African version of *Harakiri* discussed later in this chapter.

As a citizen of the British Commonwealth I come from one of those countries that require a visa to enter into the United Kingdom. One particular year I went to the British High Commission to renew my visa, something I have done effortlessly since I was a child. But that year the rules had changed. I was told that I needed two empty pages for my visa and I only had one. The visa officer said they were no longer allowed to insert a British visa at the back of a visa of another country. I needed to get a new passport before renewing my visa.

This was not good news for me. I had assumed that renewing my visa would be a seamless process and had made my travel plans based on this assumption. I had my ticket and my conference plans all confirmed. I was not amused. I had a tight timeline and I needed to get to the passport office fast, renew my passport and return to the British High Commission by the following morning. I called a friend who had renewed her passport the week before to ask for advice. She meant well. She quickly warned me: if you want your passport on time you have to pay for it. What she meant in very carefully chosen words was 'you'll have to pay a bribe'. So what started as a good day very quickly became a difficult and testy one. I knew I couldn't pay a bribe. I had taken that decision many years ago. So I sat back and thought deeply. I needed a strategy to work my way around this.

Then an idea dropped. I was reading a book at that time with a title you couldn't ignore. I felt I heard the instruction to carry the book in my hand in such a way that the title would be visible for all to read. I wish I could tell you the title of the book; unfortunately I can't remember it but trust me when I say it had a crazy title. It had the desired impact. As I went from desk to desk at the passport office, to whoever asked for a bribe I politely said, *"I am a person of faith and I don't pay bribes but I would love to pray for you. Please tell me what you need."* I wrote down what they asked for and actually stopped and prayed. I hear you laugh. Yes I looked ridiculous. But I was serious. And guess what – it worked. The passport was given to me in under three hours. The book was like a shield, a bill-board that announced my identity.

The sceptics may dismiss this story. But this is about principles and not the size of the bribe. Let me share another experience which deals with a lot more money. It was the year I was appointed to serve on the board of one of the largest banks in the country. Being the only woman on the board and by far the youngest, I took this appointment seriously. To be fully prepared for my first board meeting, a significant amount of research was done. My stomach was so tied up in knots that I couldn't even eat breakfast. At the meeting, I asked several questions that began to raise issues that showed something was not quite right. These concerns stopped an important contract from being awarded. The meeting came to an end and it was obvious that someone's plan had gone awry.

The next day I received a phone call. Someone important was coming to my house and he wanted to make sure I was home. Within 30 minutes of that phone call this Very Important Person (VIP) arrived with a really huge bag – a suitcase stuffed with money. My jaw dropped and words could not form. I ran into the bedroom to relay every single detail to my husband. The conversation ended when I clearly stated, "We need money but not this kind of money." The VIP's offer was respectfully but firmly declined. The message was clear: I could not be bought.

Did we need the money? The answer is a resounding Yes. Could I take the money? The answer was an unequivocal No.

Let us go back to the Singapore Story. At the swearing-in ceremony of Lee Kuan Yew and his cabinet they all came dressed in white – the colour of purity to represent integrity. They wanted to send a clear message to Singaporeans that it was no longer business as usual. That the core values of the nation had changed. They also wanted to state clearly that they would work as one in unity.

In his book *From Third World to First World: The Singapore Story: 1965-2000* discussed earlier in Chapter 3, there is a vivid and disturbing story of one of the ministers in the cabinet who was accused of corruption – he was suspected of taking a bribe of $81,000. The minister committed suicide. I marvel at this because of the many reports of similar charges of corruption in African states who occupy the bottom positions in terms of corruption on the Transparency International list. Many have been accused of 'stealing' millions of dollars. Very few are tried and even fewer have been jailed let alone commit suicide!

The lesson I need you to learn from this is that there is a strategy for getting around every situation that demands a bribe. If you can't get around it, walk away from it, even if it means walking away from millions of dollars. This is a war we are fighting. We are fighting for the heart and soul of our nations. We are fighting against the cancer of corruption and we can no longer afford to be half-hearted about our stance. Compromise is not on the table. This is why this is a war you cannot fight alone. You need to be part of an army that is forcefully advancing. An army that will stand with you and fight with you. That army needs to arise and take its place in communities and nations.

Undeniable Hard Work

The third leg of the stool – the third attribute is **undeniable hard work**. Hard work is often painful. It is easier to enjoy the good things of life than to work hard. It demands your time, convenience and energy. I have come to discover that the engine room for the fulfilment of dreams is hard work. Colin Powell, a former United States Secretary of State and a retired four-star general in the United States Army said, *"A dream doesn't become reality through magic; it takes sweat, determination and hard work."*

In several countries in Africa the get rich quick syndrome is prevalent and even celebrated. A generation of rent seekers has emerged who are satisfied with being middle men that take advantage of an imperfect and corrupt system. It is time to shift emphasis from easy money to hard work. Pope Paul VI stated, *"All life demands struggle. Those who have everything given to them become lazy, selfish, and insensitive to the real values of life. The very striving and hard work that we so constantly try to avoid is the major building block in the person we are today."*

Can people vouch for your integrity and your honesty? For people to attest to these qualities in you,

you need to develop the ability to stand and remain standing against all odds. This is not easy. It requires not having a Plan B if Plan A does not work out. Plan B in this situation is the easier option, the cop-out option. It also demands that in certain circumstances you may have to give up perceived rights and privileges.

No Plan B

It is not everyone that has the capability not to cave in. I see it as an outward manifestation of an inner strength. When you don't have a Plan B you have within you the ability to withstand pressure and undue hardship rather than buckle under the pressure. This is something sadly missing in many of us but is a required quality in a reformer. As mentioned earlier, it is time for the African version of *Harakiri*. Back in Ancient Rome, committing suicide by falling on one's sword became an actual practice. The Japanese samurai custom took it to another level as it became an act of great honour to commit suicide by disembowelment with a sword rather than face the dishonour of surrender. In England it became an expression that was widely used following the resignation of Lord Peter Carrington who resigned from his post as Foreign Secretary for the Thatcher government in 1982. He was one of the last high-profile politicians in the United Kingdom to take personal responsibility in such circumstances.

I remember I offered to 'fall on my sword' for the first time in early 2004. I made a grievous mistake as the head of one of the key divisions in one of the largest banks in the country. The uproar that followed that mistake was deafening and it was not going away. All the good work that we had done as a division over the previous 12 months was about to be obliterated by this singular error. I refused to make excuses; I felt I needed to take full responsibility for the incident. I was ready to walk away and to fall on my sword. This was not going to be easy as this was a job I loved. I had just finished a Master's programme at a leading world-class business school and was invited back to this financial institution to be one of the key players in a management turnaround – an opportunity that does not come often in one's career.

I offered to 'fall'. The offer was rejected. The then Chief Executive Officer stood up for me and the matter was resolved.

In another situation in an organisation I will not mention I was asked to do something that could severely affect the board if I didn't do it. If I did it I would be in the good books of the institution and be offered a promotion to a very senior position. I was at a crossroads. I asked for an hour. It was an hour to reflect and to think deeply about my values, about my beliefs, about what I stood for and believed in. I returned after that hour and offered to fall on my sword. This time I fell – I was asked to leave the organisation.

Giving Up Rights and Privileges

Recent occurrences show that we as Africans need to be ready to give up rights and privileges if need be to maintain the *Gold Standard of Non-negotiable Character Traits*. In early 2016 news broke over the world's biggest data leak – the Panama Papers. The UK *Guardian* newspaper described it as an unprecedented leak of 11.5 million files from the database of the world's fourth biggest offshore law firm, Mossack Fonseca. The firm is Panamanian but runs a worldwide operation that includes incorporating companies in offshore jurisdictions and operating in tax havens such as Switzerland, Cyprus and the British Virgin Islands. The records were obtained from an anonymous source by the German newspaper *Suddentsche Zeitung,* which shared them with the International Consortium of Investigative Journalists (ICIJ). The ICIJ then shared them with a large network of international partners, including the *Guardian* newspaper.

The documents show the myriad ways in which the rich can exploit secretive offshore tax regimes. As the news broke, the Prime Minister of Iceland, Sigmunder Davio Gunnlaugsson, resigned. Shortly after, Spain's Minister of Industry, José Manuel Soria, resigned saying that he stepped down because of *"the succession of mistakes committed along the past few days, relating to my explanations over my business activities…and considering the obvious harm that this situation is doing to the Spanish government."*

These two political leaders resigned over serious allegations of dishonest and inappropriate behaviour casting aspersions on their integrity. In Africa several top political leaders were also named in the Panama Papers – from presidents, senate leaders to ministers. None resigned.

We have to be ready to stand for what we are willing to die for. A life of no compromise is not a walk in the park. It will cost you something – your reputation, your job, your life.

It also brings you great reward – remember Nelson Mandela or William Wilberforce.

Good Character is one of the keys that unlocks the door to greatness. Greatness speaks of the extraordinary. When one is adjudged to be great it means the person has done what others have not done; he or she has acted in ways that sets them apart and distinguishes them. The lifestyle of greatness looks and 'smells' different. It takes years of consistently behaving in a distinguishing way. Years of doing something significant that marks you. It takes discipline and commitment to a cause. What do Mahatma Gandhi and Mother Theresa have in common? Their remarkable character and great deeds. What are you known for?

Finally remember – personal transformation precedes national transformation. This point is vital. Unless you are first transformed you cannot engage with national transformation. You cannot pick up a burden for a *wrong* in a nation and nurture the desire to do something about it if you cannot stand without buckling under pressure. The transformation from the inside is what leads to action on the outside.

The change that needs to take place inside of you releases what I call the 'roar of the lion'. The lion, called the King of the Jungle, has three qualities that we should desire as reformers: Courage, Boldness and Fearlessness. Grow in these qualities and you will stand out.

You Have to Be Good at It!

The second hallmark of a reformer is competence. The ability to exhibit professional competence in the sphere of society you feel called to transform. A simple dictionary definition of the word competence is *'the ability to do something successfully and efficiently'*. The Business Dictionary defines it as *'a cluster of related abilities, commitments, knowledge, and skills that enable a person (or an organisation) to act effectively in a job or situation'*. Competence indicates sufficiency of knowledge and skills that enable someone to act effectively in a wide variety of circumstances.

Many individuals deliver a product or service at a level that is often less than acceptable. They make excuses and then attempt to convince others to accept the shoddy work done. There are examples of badly tiled bathrooms, badly made furniture, badly delivered service. This failure to deliver competence becomes dangerous when it is observed in professions responsible for lives such as nursing and medicine, and for training the next generation, such as teaching.

A study carried out by the Education Support Programme in Nigeria (ESSPIN) evaluated the quality of teachers in three states in Nigeria. ESSPIN is a partnership between the United Kingdom Department for International Development (DFID) and the Nigerian government. The programme which started in 2007 supports the Federal Ministry of Education and six state governments to develop effective planning, financing and delivery systems that will improve the quality of schools, teaching and learning. The study, which evaluated the competence of teachers, was an attempt to collect baseline data that would drive the design of appropriate holistic and integrated solutions. The results from the baseline study were alarming as a significant number of the teachers were not able to answer questions meant for Grade 3-6 students. The study drew attention to the quality of the products of teacher training colleges in Nigeria.

ESSPIN has shown that for schools to be transformed into dynamic learning environments many things need to happen simultaneously. There need to be changes in the educational system as a whole, such as fundamental improvements in educational management, teaching skills, school infrastructure and learning materials. There also need to be changes beyond the school, for example in education funding and governance structures, and in the social and cultural attitudes of parents and communities.

The initial results also drew attention to the need to design another programme with specific focus on teacher development. This new programme, situated in three northern states, has the vision of raising *committed teachers with the knowledge and skills to improve the quality of learning.* The goal is to develop a new generation of competent teachers.

Many of us in our growing years experienced competent and incompetent teachers. We have also experienced shoddy work and excellent service. So the question that arises in one's mind is what makes an individual competent? What separates a competent person from an incompetent one?

Competence: The Convergence of Four Qualities

Competence can be described as the convergence of four key qualities: superior knowledge, innate and acquired skills, core values and a sterling attitude.

The Hedgehog principle in Jim Collins' book *Good to Great: Why Some Companies Make the Leap and Others Don't* states clearly what one's goal should be: to be the best at what one is good at. To be the best you have to create time to acquire knowledge and hone your skills in a deliberate and intentional way. Malcolm Gladwell in his book *Outliers* names it the 10,000 hour rule. He says that it takes roughly 10,000 hours of practice to achieve mastery in a field. To become world-class at a particular sport, musical instrument or art, he found that carrying out the action over and over again until you put in 10,000 hours gets you to a level of competency that makes you stand out. He illustrates this very clearly by citing the research by a team of psychologists that studied violin students in the 1990s in Berlin.

They studied the practice habits of these violin students in childhood, adolescence, and adulthood. All of the participants in the research were asked this question: "Over the course of your entire career, ever since you first picked up the violin, how many hours have you practised?" All of the violinists began playing at roughly five years of age with similar practice times. However, at age eight, practice times began to diverge. By age 20, the elite performers averaged more than 10,000 hours of practice each, while the less able performers had only 4,000 hours of practice. The elite had more than doubled the practice hours of the less capable performers.

As Raymond Hightower in his article on the Outlier observed: *"One fascinating point of the study: No 'naturally gifted' performers emerged. If natural talent had played a role, we would expect some of the 'naturals' to float to the top of the elite level with fewer practice hours than everyone else. But the data showed otherwise. The psychologists found a direct statistical relationship between hours of practice and achievement. No shortcuts. No naturals."*

The Journey to Becoming Competent: The Things You Need to Do

So where do you start as a young reformer? I see several action steps you can take immediately. *First, make the decision to be the best!* The best in class for knowledge. The best in class for skills. The best in class in respect of values and attitude. There are certain skills that are almost mandatory for a reformer. The ability to write objectively and communicate effectively through various mediums. The ability or skills to think critically, formulate strategy, manage people and manage projects. At another level which is becoming increasingly important is the development of social and emotional skills. Socially competent reformers know how to co-operate with each other, be helpful to others, understand their own feelings and the feelings of others and know how to resolve problems on their own. All these are part of the repertoire of skills that make you more effective.

Second, take the decision to equip yourself. Become a lifelong learner. One of the buzz words of the 21st century is 'lifelong learning'. But for a reformer these words are not buzz words. It is important you create a lifestyle of learning. You never stop reading, researching, listening or watching. Develop a mindset of discovery and adventure. Take responsibility for your own journey of lifelong learning. Learning in the 21st century is easier than ever before. There are numerous online training and equipping programmes now available. Avail yourself of what is freely available.

There is a remarkable woman I know who has reached the top of her career as a medical doctor. She was a co-owner of a private clinic for almost two decades and is now establishing an organisation that has the key objective of educating the poor on health issues. She and her reform team take complex medical issues and break each down in simple terms using the media to freely teach those who cannot afford to receive the education that will save their lives. This woman has a goal of doing a course on Coursera or Udemy every quarter. Both of these are online learning platforms structured to provide innovative learning experiences at minimal cost and sometimes at no cost. Udemy, for instance, has available over 40,000 courses taught by expert instructors, and every course is available on demand so students can learn at their own pace, in their own time and on any device.

In business school I recall the advice given of reading a book a week, and if not realistic because of one's commitment, a least a book a month.

As an enabling tool it is important to create a template of required skills for your chosen sphere and truthfully do an assessment of what skills you have and do not have. Then it is important you create a plan to address the gaps.

The third step you can take is to surround yourself with the best. Seek a community of competent people that you can be a part of and work with. This is like an athlete training for the Olympics. To be the best, the athlete cannot afford to run with anyone less than the best or else he or she will be ill-prepared to win on the big day when it matters most. Look for people with your level of passion and commitment to excellence. Look for people who are not daunted by what it takes to be the best in class. You cannot afford to resent or be envious of those you perceive to be better or more competent than you. The spirit of a reformer is not competitive. It is honouring, it applauds and celebrates others.

Closely tied to this is the *fourth step – developing a lifestyle of excellence.* Excellence is not perfection and it does not happen overnight. It is a commitment to being outstanding or extremely good. Doing your 'life work' excellently comes at a price. What you do with your time and how you deliver on your goals will determine your level of competence. Channels Television is an independent news TV channel in Nigeria founded in 1992 that started as a dream in the hearts of two outstanding broadcasters – John and Sola Momoh. Two decades later Channels TV has won the Television

Station of the Year Award for a record 10 times, five of them consecutively. This makes Channels TV the most awarded television station in Africa. They raised the bar in television broadcasting and stayed true to their vision and mission. They hired the best and invested in their development. They took being excellent in what they do very seriously and pursued it until they achieved it. This television station is the first point of reference and confirmation of breaking news stories in Nigeria, by Nigerians, and Africans in diaspora.

The fifth step which is like the glue that ties all this together is hard work. You can take the decision to be the best but if you do not put in the hard work and you are not disciplined, self-motivated and able to exercise self-control, the dream of becoming best in class will remain just that – a dream. Remember the 10,000 hour practice rule!

The Discipline of Execution: Becoming Good at the *Art of Doing*

One of Africa's banes is the poor quality of leadership. In many African nations it has been abysmal. One of the areas we are weakest at is our ability to execute. As I mentioned earlier, I served three Ministers of Education over a period of five years. This experience opened a window of opportunity to see how government works and I was able to observe the endemic struggle many have to contend with on a daily basis to get the job done.

It is not about *talking* but about *doing*. Not everyone has the ability to execute and achieve results. Lawrence Bossidy and Ram Charan in their book *Execution – the Discipline of Getting Things Done* assert that '*getting results is an outcome of the consistent practice of the discipline of execution*'. Learning how to get things done and making things happen is a skill that you can learn and it will do you good to learn this early. So let me share a simple approach, a five-step process that yields results:

1. Identify the task or project. Give it a name. When you give a name to something – an activity or even an object – it receives 'life'. It becomes a substance that you can describe, that you can shape. By naming it, the task or project now holds you accountable! It demands your attention until you accomplish or abort it. The more tasks or projects you execute, the better you get at the art of execution. It is all about discipline and practice.

2. Break the task or project into sub-tasks and clearly write down all the action steps. What is written is not forgotten. It also gives you a comprehensive to-do list that you will find invaluable. This to-do list is like erecting signposts that point in the direction you need to go. They are like the markers on a map that lead you to a desired destination.

3. Identify what you need to complete the task: the time you need to allocate to it; the *skills* you

require; the *resources* required in terms of people whose help you need; and if applicable, the seed money to fund the project or task.

4. Hold yourself accountable. Surround yourself with people who will support and encourage you. Develop zero tolerance for missed tasks. Don't be too hard on yourself but at the same time don't get complacent.

5. Collaborate if you need to in order to get things done – it strengthens the process. Chapter 7 on Collaboration discusses what I call true collaboration.

It takes more than passion to change the course of history

The Singapore Story which I first mentioned in Chapter 4 has its roots of success in a political leadership and public service that were good at what they did. They delivered excellence rooted in knowledge and understanding. When Lee Kuan Yew became prime minister in 1959 one of the first things he did was to take the decision to learn from the best. He and his leadership team left the shores of Singapore and went to the best institutions of higher learning (Oxford University and Harvard University) and consulted with the best brains. They studied development issues and possible solutions; they asked questions and enhanced their understanding. They had limited resources so as ministers and leaders who governed a newly independent nation they shared rooms and some slept on the floor to save costs. Today Singapore has the leading public service training institution – they do what they do really well. Fortune 500 companies seek to set up their Asian corporate headquarters in this nation state because of the quality of their human capital.

Dr Oby Ezekwesili is a woman who has led a life of integrity rooted in obedience. As a Special Adviser to then President of Nigeria, General Olusegun Obasanjo, she was behind a new Due Process mechanism, an instrument of public accountability that would enhance transparency in public finance and budgeting. She became known as 'Madam Due Process'. Her next appointment was Minister of Solid Minerals, followed by Minister of Education. At the end of President Obasanjo's second term in 2007, Dr Ezekwesili was head hunted and appointed Vice-President for the World Bank's Africa Region. Oby Ezekwesili has come to be recognised as a voice for the 'public good'. A woman of impact, a reformer. She is known in Africa for her passion for social justice but what distinguishes her is her intellectual prowess and knowledge of technical and social issues.

You need insight into solutions. You need to understand how to present your opinions intelligently and to craft new ways of doing things. You cannot birth change if you do not have a clear and deep understanding of the issues plaguing your sector or sphere.

Let us examine the Education Reform Team again. This is a team of professional education specialists who came together in 2011 to organise the Cross River Education Summit held in November of that year. Bound by a common vision of reforming education in Africa, the Education Reform Team partnered with forward-thinking national and state governments to execute transformation projects. Every team member is known for her or his professional competence in their area of specialisation. They have served on presidential and other high-level committees. Some own schools and others have helped to set up and turn around schools and school systems.

Each member of the team is a specialist in one or more of the six spheres of education: Early Childhood education, Basic education, Secondary School education, Tertiary education, Vocational education and Special education. Each member also has a deep understanding of the cross-cutting issues: poor quality teacher education and development, outdated curriculum development, inadequate instructional materials, poorly conceived policies, and poorly managed public educational systems to mention a few. To be a member of the Education Reform Team you need to be a person of character passionate about reform, a respected education specialist with a track record of successful projects.

I hope you are beginning to see the bigger picture as a young reformer. You need to grow in knowledge – and as you do so you grow in impact. Passion can only take you so far.

CHAPTER SIX

It is About Influence

The third hallmark of a reformer is influence. It takes influence to shift cultures. The ability to change what people believe, change how they behave and change how they do things takes a special quality. One of the better known definitions of influence comes from John Maxwell who states that the true measure of leadership is influence. Many of us have met people whose one sentence in a meeting can shift the direction of the meeting. We have also met people who talk and talk and hardly anyone agrees with what they are saying. The first, who with one sentence shifts a meeting, can be said to be a person who has influence. The other – the talker – would be judged to have less influence. Sociologists have discovered that even the most introverted individual will influence 10,000 other people during his or her lifetime.

Nicky Gumbel, a favourite speaker of mine, wrote: *'History is in many ways a story of influence. We all influence one another in all sorts of ways – from what to have for lunch and what films to watch, to more important matters of truth and ethics. As the African proverb puts it: If you think you're too small to make a difference, you haven't spent the night with a mosquito. The mosquito makes a difference in an annoying way, but the principle is the same. One person can stop a great injustice. One person can be a voice for truth. One person's kindness can save a life. Each person matters.'*

In this chapter I would like to push the boundary and explore the kind of influence that transforms the culture of a sphere, a community or a nation. The kind of influence reformers need to seek so their lives have meaningful impact. I assume this is why you are reading this book. You want to infuse into your life the *extra* in the 'extra-ordinary'. The *super* in the 'super-natural'.

One day I 'woke up' and I was tired of the ordinary. Unfortunately, by the time I woke up half my life on earth was already gone. I don't want you to wake up too late and not have enough time to do very much. This is an awakening call to the next generation to become extra-ordinary and operate in the super-natural.

My second daughter loves super heroes even though she is in her twenties. I don't understand the love she has for them but I am beginning to see in her the desire to do more than she can naturally do. I see the desire for the extra-ordinary burning within her. What I desperately want to see is an army of young people arising and burning ferociously for an extraordinary life. An army of young people who believe they can walk on water; who believe they can change their world; who believe that absolutely nothing is impossible. An army of young people who believe that their combined effort can turn their nation around and lead to the emergence of a First World Africa.

If you believe, then get up and begin to do what it takes to get influence. You can be the best in class but end up doing very little if you don't apply your best to influence change and birth transformation. So it is time to get up! Where do you start?

It starts by knowing who you are, knowing your messages, identifying your gifts and understanding timing. You recognise the timing of opportunities and you grab them.

Know Your Identity

Who Are You? I don't want to know your name. I want to know your identity. They are two different things. Knowing your identity is a journey – a journey of self-discovery. You need to *know which* part of the body you are so you can function well. You need to *know what* your assignment is so you can do it well and you need to *know who* you are meant to align with so you can impact well.

Like all journeys, the journey of self-discovery does not happen overnight. As you activate your curiosity and ask the right questions, the answers come. You hear certain words and there is an explosion in your inner being. You meet certain people and there is a quickening, a recognition. You find some tasks easy to do and others things difficult or just most unenjoyable.

So who are you? I asked myself that question many years ago. It was the beginning of my journey of self-discovery. What brought great joy? What could I do easily? What did I find difficult? What part of the body am I?

I slowly realised that I had the uncanny ability to know what I would be doing in, say, six months from a given date. I would imagine it and work towards making it happen. Today, therefore, I can tell you that I am *an eye* – often 'seeing' beyond what others see.

I also learned on my journey of self-discovery that I love to connect and introduce people. I just know instinctively who needs to meet who. I now know that I am a bridge – I connect people with those who will affect their destiny. I am what Malcolm Gladwell in his book *Tipping Point* calls a 'connector'.

I also realised that being African was a big deal for me. I am *proudly* African. At the London Business School during the Sloan Masters Programme in 2001 I felt I was representing Africa as an ambassador. Therefore I act like an ambassador – what I say and do matters. I am an ambassador for integrity. I am also a *Voice* – I create with words and release new sounds.

Lastly, after years of always starting new projects I now know I am a foundation layer – I lay the foundation for new structures that others may build beautiful edifices upon. As I walk in this identity I take what I 'see', *communicate* it to those I am *connected* with, and we now build together that which we all see. We build with the core values of love and excellence undergirding our structures. We build with the intention of changing lives and communities.

I hope the process I just described is making you curious.

So who are you? I asked a group of 12 people that question a few years ago. Each one was to write their answer from their understanding of the question. Eleven of them gave their names, told me they were wives, mothers etc. Only one person answered the question from the deeper perspective. Only one said with great confidence, "*I am a midwife. I facilitate the birthing of dreams.*"

Today I ask you the same question – **Who Are You?** I encourage you to think before you answer.

Know Your Message

Know your message and proclaim it with passion and intentionality. Articulate your message in your own words. Be authentic. Being authentic is now one of those buzz words used by business school gurus but it is actually an important quality. One of those important qualities that good leaders must learn to embrace. Be real and genuine, be an original don't be a copy, be true and accurate, be your true *you*.

Many of us understand the importance of words. Words are powerful, they create. The spoken word releases an energy that transforms atmospheres. With words you can create an atmosphere of love, anger, hatred or compassion. With words you can effect change in behaviours and change in actions. With words you shape the character of individuals – you can build or destroy. Words can carry an innate power that explodes on impact.

You can build 'physical' structures with words. You have the power to build an edifice – defined as '*a building, especially one of large size or imposing appearance*' – with just words. With the right words the 'building' (your organisation) can look solid and imposing. It can look attractive and irresistible and attract the resources required – human and financial resources. This is why as a reformer your use of words must be deliberate, intentional and full of wisdom. A wisdom that catches people's attention is not the usual wisdom – it is a gift of wisdom that you should seek.

As a reformer you must not take vision statements and written plans for granted. Do not write them nonchalantly as mere words. They have creative powers and have the ability to build your future and create a pathway to significance. They can redefine your destiny and guide you to purpose. Your words can explode on a page; they can release rain when a refreshing is needed. Words re-create worlds.

Richard Branson and the Virgin Group have mastered the use of words and media to create an identity and customer experiences that is unique. People are willing to pay for Richard Branson's unique selling proposition which is Virgin. A brand that catered to the 'hip' GenX who wanted something different. The play on words that Virgin uses to advertise guarantees that you never forget their advertisements.

Mark McClures of the Ruthless Entrepreneur states, *"If you can define your vision, define your goals and clearly define what it is you do (your message), how you do it and WHY you do it, the world will become your oyster."*

The authentic **YOU** has a message to proclaim. One of the most authentic people that I know is Christine Caine, author of *Undaunted, Unstoppable* and recently *Unashamed*. She is also an outstanding speaker and the co-founder of A21 – a global organisation she and her husband set up in 2008. The A21 campaign is dedicated to addressing the injustice of human trafficking in the 21st century. A21's comprehensive approach includes awareness, preventing future trafficking, taking legal action, and offering support services to survivors.

Christine with her spoken and written words is declaring a loud message that says a resounding *NO* to human trafficking and 21st century slavery. She is known for her ability to communicate very clearly, profound messages of hope, inspiration and freedom.

Know Your Gifts

Many go through life without knowing their gifts. Our attention is on gifts and not talent. Becoming more self-aware helps you understand your gifts. What comes to you easily? What brings you joy? What do you struggle doing? There is a leading specialist in the medical field that I know who has the gift of **wisdom**. She was listed in the 2007/2013 Tatler's Guide to Britain's 250 best private doctors. When she speaks people listen. She sees with uncanny clarity and a deep understanding of solutions to problems. She started noticing that people at meetings would stop talking and seek her opinion before taking decisions. It took her 25 years to realise that she had the gift of wisdom. This gift enhances your ability to know what to do, when to do it and how to do it. In summary, you become a good strategist.

Another gift is **foresight** defined as *'the ability to predict what will happen or be needed in the future'*. People with foresight are able to anticipate, prepare and plan more effectively. Add to this the gift of **insight** which is *'the capacity to gain an accurate and deep understanding of someone or something'* and you become a strong reformer. A person with these gifts is usually visionary and yet understands the details of making things happen. They can bring these gifts to bear in policy formulation, recognising business opportunities, addressing injustice, fighting for a cause, and designing strategic programmes. These are just a few of the gifts that can enhance who you are. Others include the gift to administer, the gift to counsel and coach. Begin to track what comes to you easily. Track what you can do effortlessly. Identify your gift and learn to work and enhance it.

Understand the Times

Great influencers know the power of timing. They do the right thing in the right season at the right time.

When you live on a continent that experiences the four seasons – spring, summer, autumn and winter – you learn to modify your behaviour and your dressing to suit the seasons. No one in their right mind would come out on a blustery, bitterly cold winter morning in their swimming gear. Neither would you wear a furry winter coat on a hot summer day with beautiful blue skies. We dress appropriately for the season. Likewise as someone who seeks to understand the seasons and the times, you need to learn to discern the change in the seasons of your life as you live through time. You learn to be sensitive, you learn to adjust your behaviour, you learn what to do at the right time. When you get timing right you are always better prepared.

Let me share a personal experience. My appointment as Head of Human Capital Management of a large bank was terminated suddenly, without warning. But instead of going into despair I actually walked out thoroughly pleased with the decision. I gave a Victory sign as I walked out of the meeting where I was given the news. Why? The decision did not catch me off-guard. I was expectant because I knew the season had changed.

Rewind to two years prior to my termination. I had just finished the Sloan Masters programme at the London Business School (LBS), an international business school founded in 1964. LBS is one of the most prestigious business schools in the world; the school is ranked 1st in Europe (2015 rankings) by the *Financial Times* and 2nd in the world (for Business and Management studies, 2016) by the QS ranking. The motto of the school is *'To have a profound impact on the way the world does business'.*

So here I was at the end of my Sloan Masters Programme feeling exhilarated and ready to conquer the business world! I felt empowered and I knew I could pursue any number of opportunities. The first that presented itself was to go back to the bank I worked with before going to LBS. They were offering me an exciting new position as part of a turnaround team. The second opportunity was to partner with another LBS student and set up a private equity firm together. I was torn but I finally took the decision to take the offer with the bank because the turnaround project sounded so exciting. Also I clearly heard a 'still small voice' tell me that I would be there for only 12-18 months (note the timing). So my rational mind thought that perhaps I could still join the private equity firm after 18 months.

The first year back at the bank was one of the best years I have ever had working in an organisation. I had the opportunity to apply a lot of what I learned in business school. The course on Managing Turnarounds was one of my favourite courses. We learned that a major source of increasing revenues almost immediately after a turnaround team steps into an organisation is to institute cost-saving measures. As the new head of the Human Capital department I was given the mandate to reduce my team from 120 to under 40 people. We were not asking them to leave the organisation, we just had to re-assign many of them to the market-facing business units within the bank. This singular action reduced the costs of the HR department by 50% and increased the revenue potential of the branches.

A second major task was to significantly reduce the electricity bill of the head office from N10m (ten million Naira) a month to N1m (one million Naira). We were haemorrhaging money through the inefficient use of power. A few simple adjustments yielded significant results. We issued guidelines that mandated switching off equipment and light switches at the end of the day. Before then the head office looked like a lit-up Christmas tree with everyone leaving unnecessary lights on. Then we removed refrigerators from individual offices and centralised them so that one refrigerator now served at least eight people instead of each senior person having one to themselves. The policy at that time was that as soon as you became a principal manager you got a fridge. So in one section of the office where you had four principal managers sitting in a corner you had four fridges. From the HR department alone we took out over 27 fridges.

Sixteen months after this exciting work started, all hell broke loose. I was requested to take certain actions that did not resonate with my professional values. I refused and actually wanted to resign but kept getting the feeling that I was not to walk out but to wait. So in obedience I waited and my appointment was terminated in the 18th month. As I was prepared for the possibility of this event happening (remember the 'still small voice' that told me about timing) I celebrated my exit instead of being traumatised by it. Also, because I waited and did not resign, I got a huge significant pay-off. If I had resigned I would have had to pay outstanding loans and benefits. I had the patience to wait because I knew the season was changing in the 18th month.

Understanding timing is one of the marks of a reformer. This is why we cannot but appreciate the gay movement and the progress they have made in influencing the culture of today and the thinking of people. A minority group with careful planning and an understanding of timing has used media to affect cultures and create change. What was not permissible in one generation is now permissible. Amongst other factors, they understand the times.

> *"A man without the discernment of time is walking in the dark."* - **Sunday Adelaja**

We have discussed ways of enhancing your influence by knowing who you are, knowing your gifts and your message, and knowing what to do at the appropriate time. All of this has the combined effect of announcing and strengthening your 'voice' of influence. In the next section we will examine the qualities of influence.

The Qualities of Influence

Influence has two qualities – it has a *Sound* and it has *Purpose*. These qualities can be amplified and enhanced by the actions you take.

The Sound of Influence

The sound of influence is bold, fearless and courageous. In Chapter 1 we looked at reformers as sound shapers. In the 21st century the sound of influence can be magnified by social media. Therefore the quality of your message and the sound it carries is important. It is not the noise you make.

Social media has become a platform where you can use words to distinguish yourself. Not empty words but words full of wisdom and purpose. Words that create a following and give you influence. You have the opportunity to shape thoughts and actions. Oby Ezekwesili, whom we mentioned earlier, has influence on Twitter that has undoubtedly grown in significant leaps. In 12 months her Twitter following has grown from 200,000 to 483,200 followers (140% increase). Her profile describes her as *'a fiercely passionate believer in the public good of nations, serving before leading. Validated by God and my Dad who taught me to never dignify nonsense.'* A Thought Leader who cannot be ignored, she expresses strong views on important political and social issues. She is co-founder of the Bring Back Our Girls Campaign, now a global movement that witnessed the involvement of Michelle Obama, David Cameron, Malala Yousafzai, famous Hollywood actors like Sylvester Stallone and stars at the Cannes Festival in 2014, each one carrying the sign reading #Bring Back Our Girls.

Keep your message on social media simple and clear. Keep it strong and meaningful. As you focus on impacting others it will get louder. Sound has vibrations and the quality of your vibration is measured by what it shakes. Higher vibrations = greater impact. There is a sound that comes from one that has experienced sacrifice and death. A life that has emptied itself releases a purity of sound that cannot be ignored.

Influence Has Purpose

Influence is not just for the sake of influence. It is to change the narrative of a life, of a community, of a culture of a nation. Mother Teresa changed the lives of the downtrodden in India. She and her team helped those most desperately in need: lepers, unwed mothers, discarded infants, the ill, the insane, the retarded, the dying. A photographer May Ellen Mark, who once spent a month at the mission house in Calcutta, wrote: *'In this extreme of suffering, pus, blood, vomit, urine, screams, sad and vacant faces – the sisters never stop working; they are gentle and kind. Each time I ask something, the sister tells me, "It is God's work, don't you see?"'*

One of the most powerful ways to exert influence is through volunteerism, especially purposeful volunteerism. A useful definition for volunteerism is the *'practice of volunteering one's time or talents for charitable, educational, or other worthwhile activities, especially in one's community'* (www.dictionary. com). It is generally considered an altruistic activity where an individual or group provides services for no financial gain. Volunteering also serves as a great way to acquire and develop new skills. It also releases within you a spirit of love and service. Through it you often experience a dying to self, you become less self-absorbed and more other-focused. You see in more practical ways how what you do, say and think affects lives and changes individuals and communities. No volunteering experience – whether good or bad – leaves you the same!

Slum2School Africa, a volunteer-driven social development organisation that was mentioned earlier in Chapter 3, was built on the back of volunteerism. There are over 5,000 professional volunteers from 12 countries working together to rescue out-of-school children living in the slums. This young organisation has been described as one of the most vibrant youth-driven non-profit organisations in Nigeria. The work they do has received well-deserved media attention, accolades and several awards (over 15 national and international awards).

So many of us complain about the issues we face in Africa. We complain about the quality of our schools and the poorly qualified teachers. It is time to do something about it; as a graduate you can volunteer to teach. We complain about the filth and dirty environment in many of our cities; again it is time to do something about that – volunteer to clean up!

For society to change there are said to be seven 'Walls of Society' that need urgent repair. We need transformational leaders to arise and take responsibility for this repair. Some authors – Loren Cunningham, Bill Bright and Johnny Enlow to name three – call these the seven mountains or seven moulders of culture. I first encountered Loren Cunningham of Youth with a Mission through one of his books *Daring to Live on the Edge: The Adventure of Faith and Finances.* This was the first book that I ever picked up that made my palms go hot. Don't ask me how that happened. It happened. It was a sign that I had to buy the book and I did – I bought five copies.

The second person, Bill Bright, founder of Campus Crusade for Christ, I 'met' halfway across the world through someone who worked in his organisation. That person carried the spirit of this organisation so beautifully.

The third is Johnny Enlow – the only one that I have actually met – is a passionate social reformer and is the author of *The Seven Mountain Prophecy*, *The Seven Mountain Mantle* and his latest book *The Seven Mountain Renaissance*. There are seven 'mountains' or mind moulders of society, namely: media, education, government, economy/business, celebration of arts, religion, and family. If you have influence, you can shape what happens on these mountains in your nation.

These mind moulders frame the mindsets of the 21st century. The way people think, their beliefs and values. Those who wield influence are able to change the narratives of these mind moulders.

Which broken wall are you repairing? Which mountain are you taking responsibility for? Which mind moulder are you crafting a new narrative for?

Reformer Arise and take your place. Use your influence purposefully.

CHAPTER SEVEN

Reformers Do Not Work Solo - They Collaborate

The word solo is derived from the word single. Other words that describe this word include alone, unaccompanied, by yourself. A quick review of history has shown that significant landmark events or changes are often not carried out by one individual working alone. Please note that I am not referring to scientific discoveries or inventions. I wish to refer mainly to systemic socio-economic changes, mindset shifts and cultural revolutions. Very often it's a group of like-minded individuals passionate about a cause that come together and create a momentum that leads to a movement.

If this simple fact is true and easy to understand, why do so many of us believe we can make change happen alone? In my part of the world there seems to be a pervasive tendency to act alone.

The Danger of Working Solo and Initial Steps to Collaborating

In life we usually only see in part, we often do not see the whole picture. You cannot see the back of your head but someone standing behind you can. Likewise it is almost impossible to see the whole picture by yourself. Remember I mentioned earlier how each of us carries a piece of the puzzle? If you carry only a piece you cannot possibly complete the puzzle by yourself. You have to find the other pieces of the puzzle and connect with them. It is therefore often dangerous to try and work solo when you clearly cannot see the complete picture.

Where does it start? It starts with connecting and connecting takes a skill. First there has to be *recognition.* You need to have the ability to recognise that the person you are connecting with is a missing piece of the puzzle. You have your identity and the other person also has theirs. Each identity is unique and it is this differentiation that allows recognition. Secondly, you have to be *willing* to connect and to do this – humility and selflessness is required. There is no place for pride and an overblown estimation of self. Thirdly, you have to understand the *importance* of connecting. If you don't connect, the puzzle remains incomplete.

A completed puzzle is an achievement and an accomplishment. Scattered pieces of a puzzle make no sense. You cannot see the picture or understand the message that it conveys. In like manner, reformers that work solo dilute their message, appear powerless and are easily defeated. Take for example the poor educational system in many emerging countries such as those in West Africa. Many schools are failing and the public servants are grappling with the problems. You arrive on the scene as a solo consultant running your organisation. How do you address the issues of poorly trained teachers, poorly qualified inspectors, inadequate learning materials, dilapidated infrastructure – the list goes on.

Flip this and say you now arrive on the scene with a strong team – say an Education Reform Team (ERT). On that team you have specialists known for their successful track record for teacher education, designing curriculum, empowering and retraining inspectors, creating relevant cost-effective learning materials, a revolutionary design using locally available materials for building classrooms at a significantly lower cost. Each member of the ERT is good at what he or she does. Together they have formed a formidable force and exercise great influence. They have connected and the puzzle looks complete.

I am dwelling on the word 'connect' because it is a prerequisite for collaboration. Once connection happens, the other ingredients for *true collaboration* can now be added. Note the word *'true'*.

I was fortunate enough to attend business school after working for over 15 years. I felt so much had changed in the world since I did my first Masters Programme 20 years earlier. At the London Business

School I learned the importance of collaboration. How businesses succeeded because they built cultures where collaboration was encouraged and celebrated. Armed with this knowledge I entered into my first partnership in 2004. I invested in a growing firm by buying equity. Although I didn't know my new partners very well, as we worked together we got to know each other. Today we are good friends even though our business endeavour didn't work. We started off with passion and a lot of zeal but it didn't take very long before our diverse expectations and our ways of working began to show the cracks in our collaborative entity. I very quickly learned that there is a difference between the collaboration taught in business school and *true collaboration*. Two years after we signed our partnership agreement we all agreed to part ways and pursue the dreams we carried in each of our hearts.

Through this experience I learned some valuable lessons about what I now call *'true collaboration'*. I have also gleaned additional lessons and insight from being a core member of the Education Reform Team. Business school collaboration will not take reformers very far. It is not sacrificial neither is it willing to die for a cause. What differentiates *'true collaboration'* from what I learned at business school?

True Collaboration

I believe there are five simple but important differences – what I call the fundamental ingredients of *true collaboration*.

The first is foundational as it lays the foundation for the other ingredients. This is the twin emotions of *Love and Death.* They are like two sides of the same coin. You have to be able to love those you are in collaboration with unconditionally. It means no matter what they do to you, you still love and care for them and still want to work with them. This is hard – really hard. The other side of the coin is death. You have to learn to die to self. Through dying to self you learn to esteem your collaborating partners above yourself. If you are not able to pass this initial test I guarantee that your collaboration will not go beyond being a business relationship. It is not business relationship collaboration that changes nations. To fight for a cause, to change systems that have remained the same for years, to be part of a movement that shifts culture, you must be prepared to be a reformer that *loves deeply* and is *dead.*

The second fundamental ingredient is *Vision and Heart Collaboration.* It goes beyond sharing a vision that was crafted during a brainstorming weekend retreat. This is not the kind of vision that moves mountains. Reformers' hearts have to be knit together bound by a pulsating vision. A vision that refuses to let go until it is fulfilled. A vision that demands your all and the all of every true collaborating partner. Anyone that is hesitant and is counting the cost cannot operate in true collaboration. In the business world financial collaboration often comes first before heart collaboration. In the reformer's world heart collaboration precedes financial collaboration.

The third ingredient does not come easily. It is about *Giving and Sharing*. It is about giving, giving, giving and giving. You give of your resources, your time and of your future. You have an acute perception of needs and you offer to meet those needs. You never stop giving. You don't always give because you have, you learn to give from your nothingness, from your emptiness. I remember many years ago a friend who is easily one of the most generous people I know gave me an expensive study Bible that she had just purchased. I walked into her as she left the bookstore. I made the mistake of admiring the study Bible and immediately she handed it to me and said that I could have it. She could *give* anything – there was nothing she owned that she could not give away. Her husband used to jokingly say, "If she could, she would give me away." As team members give sacrificially to one another it provokes a response, an emotional connection, almost like an invisible rope that binds the hearts together.

The fourth ingredient is *Sincerity and Openness*. The tendency of human nature is to hide things. History is replete with stories of leaders who were betrayed. From the legendary Julius Caesar whose reign was ended by a coup on the Ides of March to Steve Jobs, the famous co-founder CEO of Apple who was removed as CEO by his board and forced out of Apple, the company he founded in 1985.

Once the door to doubt and insincerity is opened up, negative emotions such as back-biting and competitiveness begin to eat away at the fabric of unity that binds a people together. Truth and authenticity are key. Untruths often told to protect reputations and to avoid punishment must be frowned upon. Conversely, openness and sincerity have to be held in highest regard and rewarded.

The fifth is *Humility and Unity*. The word humility conjures different images in different people. It connotes images of being trampled upon by others if one is humble. Of being overlooked in the workplace and often missing out on promotions and other benefits that people think they have to fight for to get. In the culture of the 21st century a certain level of aggressiveness, standing up for oneself, being noticed and fighting for one's perceived rights are all acceptable behaviour. Blowing your own trumpet is often seen as quite vital to advancing in your career.

Humility can be described as *'the opposite of aggressiveness, arrogance, boastfulness and vanity. Rather than "Me first," humility allows us to say "No, you first." Humility is the quality that lets us go more than halfway to meet the needs and demands of others'* **(Patricia Hagemann).**

In his book *Good to Great: Why Some Companies Make the Leap and Others Don't*, Jim Collins discovered, through a five-year study of outstanding companies who had transitioned from being average to great companies by outperforming the stock market, that their CEO had an unusual quality as a Level-5 Leader. They each exhibited the quality of humility. This finding was unexpected. It went against the grain of what was being taught in business schools as acceptable behaviour. Humility was not one of those enviable character traits. It was at the back of this that authenticity and being authentic was seen as a highly attractive quality in a leader.

Humility strengthens unity in a partnership or a team. Unity of purpose and unity of vision maintains *true collaboration*. Unity is not unison; it allows divergent arguments without eating at the core of the unity that binds the team together. Unity is powerful and yet it is never easy. It is always a huge challenge. It is unity with a deep measure of humility that leads to victory.

The Power of Collaboration

Collaboration releases an unusual power. It is a force that cannot be easily overcome. It is the force that changes nations and shifts cultures. It is the force that propels national transformation – and that is why true collaboration comes at a price. Each member of the group has to be prepared to give himself or herself away to the cause. You are prepared to live in 'prison'; for the sake of the group you give up certain rights and privileges. There is an ethos and a deep understanding that binds you together.

The analogy of power generation and distribution is an apt representation of the message I need you to understand. As a power-generating company, if you generate power and transmission lines are not in place you cannot distribute. The power generated by collaboration is released through the members, the reformers that form the group. If the reformers are not in place the power has nowhere to go. If the reformers have 'glitches' (character issues, disunity etc.) that affects the flow of the power, that power will not reach its destination, which are the spheres of society that so desperately need that power. Reformers who understand that the source of great power is collaboration learn to give up their rights and privileges to become a formidable force in their spheres of influence.

If this is so powerful is there any wonder that there are forces that contend against collaboration? Political parties that start well fall apart. Reform teams with great vision and passion flounder.

The Forces that Contend against Collaboration

Internal and external forces contend against individuals who come together with a commitment to see change. Let us recognise these forces and contend against them. The internal forces are quietly and insidiously destructive like a cancer. External forces are often noisy, demanding attention, but I find them less destructive than the internal.

Internal forces work in two ways: inside the individual reformer and within the group. The battle within is more deadly than the battle without. Like a cancer you cannot afford to ignore it, hide it or wish it away. You confront it and you cut it off. Selfishness, self-centredness, greed, an exaggerated opinion of one's ability, 'I' versus 'We' thinking are some of the forces within each of us that destroy a group's ability to have great impact.

Within the group we have similar destructive behaviours such as competing with one another instead of learning how to co-operate; thinking of today instead of focusing on tomorrow. What can best be described as war against 'legacy thinking'.

As I write these words I feel pain. The pain of failed attempts to be the change we want to see. The pain of reform teams that started well but then fell apart, each member going their separate way and taking a piece of the dream that no longer resembles the dream they carried when they were one. I wonder sometimes if nation-building teams can arise in my home continent – Africa. Can the reformers truly die to selfish ambition? Can they refuse to be transactional players in their economies and instead become transformational in character and nature? Can they look at corruption eyeball to eyeball and say, 'I have a new DNA, I will not be seduced by you'?

What will it take to think like this? What it will take to build a culture that contends against these internal and external forces? I want to know what practical steps I can take. In 2012 as CEO of the organisation I started, I challenged my team to design a plan for an organisational culture that would instruct people in the kind of behaviour that sustains collaboration for nation building. Two strategies have emerged: what I call the Butterfly Strategy and the Doormat Strategy.

Are you ready for a journey of personal transformation? To become a reformer and part of a nation-building community, personal transformation is non-negotiable.

As I mentioned earlier in Chapter 4, you cannot be a change maker, a reformer, without a visible journey of personal transformation. Visible to you and visible to others. Your journey of transformation should be that of a caterpillar becoming a butterfly. You embrace what Tomas Premuzic and Michael Sanger call *'the core ingredients of leadership that is universal – good judgment, integrity and people skills'*. You become totally committed to doing what is right no matter the cost. You learn to be forceful and persistent and yet gentle towards those you are serving.

You often have to learn how to become a 'doormat'. Two difficult life experiences – at a personal and professional level – unveiled this strategy. To receive victory in the emotional battles of strife, malice, bitterness and unforgiveness you learn to lay your reputation down. You lay down your right to be 'right'. You lay down your reputation so that others may walk over you, and as they do so they see in you an unusual strength that brings them to a place where they admire you for your courage. As this happens, you become a sign of what a life of humility looks like. This challenges those watching to act differently and seek to be different. This journey that you choose to undertake is often painful, difficult and humiliating. But it is a choice for the greater good. You make it to bring a transforming influence to the group. As members of the group walk in the 'doormat strategy' it builds a culture of love and honour as each person esteems the other above themselves. Covenant is strengthened and the group is ready to do big things together.

Humility and esteeming others above oneself now becomes the glue that strengthens reform teams. National Transformation Networks can begin to emerge as the whole becomes more effective than individual 'kingdom' agendas.

An Organised Army: A New Community

The end goal of collaboration is to build an army of reformers – a new community that carries the vision and power to institute reform in society. This army is well organised. They do not break ranks. They have a clear understanding of their mission, of their assignment. They understand the rules of engagement and they abide by them. There is a culture that binds these 'soldiers' together. In the next chapter we shall examine this culture in greater detail and highlight stories of successful communities of change.

Building a New Community of Reformers

As we come to the end of this book, it is my hope that a burning desire to do something transformational has been birthed. A desire that burns deeply within your soul. I hope you have learned what it will take for you to become a Radical Love Carrier who is prepared to pay the price.

It is going to be hard work. It is going to be painful. We will need policy formulation specialists, legal specialists, communication and media specialists, project managers, financial experts, qualified teachers and health workers, political activists, social enterprise experts, etc. We will need reformers in every sphere of society, each with a mindset that has stepped out of the old and into the new.

This book is not a recipe for turning Third World nations into First World. It is about *You* and the role you can play as you rise up and take your place, as you get into position, as you connect with others who are crying out for change. This is why I believe we can make it happen.

But, right now, reformers are struggling. This is the truth. Paul Collier captures it beautifully by pointing out that in the countries in the bottom billion *'there are struggles between brave people wanting change and entrenched interests opposing it. It is time to do more to strengthen the hand of the reformers'.* Paul goes on to advocate, *'For our future world to be livable the heroes must win the struggle. But the villains have the guns and the money, and to date they have usually prevailed. That will continue unless we radically change our approach'.*

This book is about radically changing our approach.

Let us examine the Clapham Sect again and the impact they had on society and let's see what we can learn from their approach. Bruce Hindmarsh in his article on *William Wilberforce and the Abolition of the Slave Trade: A Gallery of Aristocratic Activists* described the Sect as *'one of the most elite and effective bands of Christian social reformers – ever'.* They were a group of well-connected and well-heeled individuals. They combined their considerable talents and expertise, religious zeal and optimism in a concerted campaign of national reform.

Beyond the abolition of slavery, they improved the quality of education given to the poor and their humanitarian ideals helped bring about a more egalitarian society. The sect pioneered techniques of mobilising public opinion that have become commonplace in democracies. They exploited the media outlets of the day: lectures, billboards, newspapers and pamphlets. They made effective use of voluntary societies and unprecedented use of petitions to exert public pressure on Parliament.

Their advocacy was marked by careful research, planning and strategy. They kept the 'long view' on completing projects – the abolition of slavery took 20 years! They enabled one another versus trying to 'have it all'. They recognised each other's passions and supported one another in addressing them. They were committed to lifelong friendship and mutual submission was the norm.

We have several significant lessons to learn from this Group:

- They had unity of purpose
- They were committed and resilient
- They demonstrated the value and power of volunteerism
- They had a strong voice (advocacy) for the less privileged
- The entire group displayed and manifested the reformer's mindset described in Chapter 2

In this Sect whenever a new cause was championed by the Clapham Friends, a society was organised to carry it out. This is a key strategy I don't want you to miss. Are we ready to establish societies – *'reform teams'* around causes and deep-seated problems?

Sustaining a Movement: Building Communities

When people become involved with *'a cause greater than them; when they start looking outward in the same direction'* something significant begins to happen. A movement begins, communities form.

To sustain this movement and build the communities, a *reformers' culture* needs to be incubated and nurtured. We need to establish a culture where reform thrives and the individual reformers have room to express their gifts and apply their knowledge and competence in a collaborative rather than competitive atmosphere. I believe there are four cultures that differentiate reformers' communities:

1. A Culture of Honour

2. A Culture of Love and Service

3. A Culture of Learning (Lifelong Learning – which we touched upon in Chapter 5)

4. A Culture of Action

A Culture of Honour

The culture of honour is like glue – it keeps the separate pieces of the puzzle together. It can be described as the cement that joins bricks together so they are impenetrable. Each reformer is a building block that stands alone. As they become part of a community, a soldier in the army, the culture of honour binds them together.

The principle of honour says that *accurately acknowledging who people are will position us to give them what they deserve and to receive the gift of who they are in our lives.* The key here is *accurately acknowledging who people are.* When we do so we will begin to value the gifts and talent each person carries. We will not look down on anyone based on their perceived outward appearance or status in life.

This is not as easy as it sounds because society has taught us to esteem ourselves above others, to consider ourselves better than others.

A community creates a culture of honour as the members of that community *learn to discern and receive people in their God-given identities.* Each person learns to say, 'You have something I don't have, and I need what you have.' Let me try to simplify this point. Many years ago, I had the opportunity of sitting in on a John Maxwell training course. Over a period of three days, I listened to many valuable principles that he taught but the one principle that struck me and has stuck with me is John Maxwell saying, *"I give a 10 to everyone I meet for the first time."* He marks their forehead with an invisible 10. That number drops below 10 or remains at 10 depending on the quality of their discussion, and more importantly, their understanding of who they are.

Everyone is honoured as they score a 10. Honour empowers people.

Honour creates an atmosphere where the community becomes a strong supportive family characterised by one singular quality – love. A loving family creates an environment that has certain ingredients that allow family members to thrive, excel, grow and express their true creative self. These ingredients are similar to what allows a tree to grow: well-watered soil with plenty of sunshine and the right nutrients.

A Reformers' Community needs to create a similar kind of environment – an environment that is non-competitive and celebrates each person's uniqueness. That allows mistakes because through mistakes, growth comes. An environment where the 'family' fights together for a common cause against a common enemy and no one is left alone in the battlefield. An environment where family sticks together and builds a united front.

A Culture of Love and Service

It was Martin Luther King Jr that said, *"Not everybody can be famous, but everybody can be great because greatness is determined through service."*

Love and honour underlie a culture of service. The strength of a Reformers' Community lies in the willingness of each reformer to serve at two levels. The first is in serving one another within the community, offering help and assistance through genuine love and care. If we are not able to care for one another, how do we care for those whose lives we wish to impact? Mother Teresa said, *"Never worry about numbers. Help one person at a time, and always start with the person nearest you."* This is the second level of service – serving *'the One'* whose life you are willing and wanting to change.

Service is doing what is not always convenient. It is giving of yourself when no one is watching and there is no self-glorification or gratification.

As part of a team I have served three Ministers of Education in the Federal Government of Nigeria over a period of five years. I have noticed that there are two types of consultants: those who struggle to work with public servants whom they often perceive as inefficient, out-of-date and incompetent, and those who serve these same public servants with understanding and a deep desire to partner with them. The outcomes of both categories of consultants are starkly different. There is tension, discomfort and a reluctance on the part of the public servants to assist and work with the first type of consultant. The converse is true for the second type who enjoy co-operation and allegiance.

The Dubai Story: A Love for a People and a Willingness to Serve

I visited Dubai for one reason: I needed to see what all the fuss was about. This was a city that in the 1950s was a small village of tents and mud huts, with a few traditional dhows moored in the muddy water of a modest creek. Today it is a city that has experienced spectacular growth and amazing development. This tiny emirate has raised its profile globally through a range of bold developments and clever ideas: the free zones for business that have made it a regional centre for many firms; the Dubai international airport; the world famous ports; the Dubai International Financial centre; the most stunning hotels in the world including the Burj Al Arab (the world's only 'seven-star' hotel) – the list goes on.

These bold developments created a phenomenon, described as a 'strategic vortex' by Saab Eigner and Jeffrey Sampler in their Book *Sand to Silicon: Achieving Rapid Growth Lessons from Dubai*. The sheer magnitude and speed of development creates a momentum that makes development unstoppable. This strategic vortex creates a springboard for future development and significant asset creation leading to continuously greater shipping capacity, more free zones, more hotels and more of the spectacular.

A phrase that caught my attention in this book is the observation that *'there is a strong bond between the people of Dubai and the ruling Al Maktoum family'*. This is a leadership that loves and honours its people. When Dubai's visionary Crown Prince, Sheikh Mohammed, was interviewed, he said his responsibility was to ensure a delicate balance between Dubai's growth and its culture and tradition. A love for a people and a willingness to serve them is key to building a community that drives change.

Culture of Learning – Lifelong Learning

Finnish education first received global attention in 2003 when it ranked No. 1 in the PISA study. The Programme for International Student Assessment (PISA) is a worldwide study by the Organisation for Economic Co-operation and Development (OECD) in member and non-member nations of 15-year-old school pupils' scholastic performance in mathematics, science and reading. Finland was first in both science and reading and second in mathematics. In addition, the country's tertiary education has been ranked 1st by the World Economic Forum. The world was shocked. What exactly was Finland doing to yield such phenomenal results?

On the back of these amazing achievements, the Education Reform Team went on a Learning Journey to Finland in 2012. We discussed the lessons learnt in Chapter 3. Relevant for this section is Finnish education's strong emphasis on lifelong learning. The aim is to consistently improve knowledge, skills and competences within a personal, civic, social and employment-related space. No one is encouraged to leave the school system. There are several bridges connecting one level to another for those who miss the opportunity as children, teenagers or young adults. The Finnish educational system has a well-defined lifelong learning ecosystem that makes learning enjoyable and rewarding.

Fred Swaniker in a recent article *Go back to school – or go obsolete* described what he called 'just in time' (JIT) education and mentioned three characteristics. I will mention two here:

1. It never ends. University used to be an institution you attended for four years and the training received was supposed to last for the next 40 years of your career. Fred says this may have worked 40 years ago, but in the JIT education world you continue learning for your whole life. Through such lifelong learning, you keep reinventing yourself to stay relevant as the world changes.

2. It focuses far less on facts and figures and instead on learning how to learn. The aim is to make you extremely comfortable with change. Fred observes that the facts and figures are a means to an end, they are not the end. The 'end' is to acquire a set of 'meta-skills' like how to work in teams, how to communicate, how to solve problems, how to analyse data, how to think critically, how to lead, and how to think entrepreneurially. These, he says, are the skills that will remain relevant even as the world changes.

The 21st century learning environment is one that makes lifelong learning much easier to attain. Access to the wealth of information on the internet has reached mega proportions.

Rotimi Williams, the 35-year-old entrepreneur who owns Nigeria's second largest rice farm, recently received a great deal of media attention. His farm is situated in Northern Nigeria in Nasarawa State and sits on 45,000 hectares, employing more than 600 indigenes. I found it interesting that Rotimi attended King's College in Lagos, Nigeria – the same secondary school my brothers attended. After King's College he proceeded to obtain his first degree at the University of Aberdeen where he graduated with a degree in Economics. He got a Master's Degree in Economics from the same university. A few years later he enrolled for yet another Master's Degree at the School of Oriental and African Studies, London where he got an MSc in Finance and Development Studies.

Rotimi started his working career in the financial services industry but was drawn into agriculture. He went into farming and by sheer determination and passion he now owns the second largest commercial rice farm in his country. When asked how he learned about farming, as many think one needs a special degree in agriculture to be a farmer, Rotimi says, "*I always tell them the truth, I learnt it all on Google. I downloaded every article I could find on rice production, consumed it and then practised it in the fields.*"

A reformer's mindset is constantly refreshed and renewed by new knowledge and new skills. It is a mindset that is inquisitive and by staying at the cutting edge of information, it stays relevant and sought after.

In the academic world the powerful collaboration that characterises professional learning communities is a systematic process in which teachers work together to analyse and improve their classroom practice. It increases educator effectiveness and results of students.

Transpose this in a Reformers' Community and you have a pretty powerful experience taking place. Solution carriers that work together as reform teams can use their collective knowledge and experiences to design strong, holistic, integrated programmes with lasting impact. Like compound interest, the knowledge of each reformer is compounded as they work together to solve societal problems. The DNA that makes this work is an atmosphere of respect and esteeming others above oneself. There is no room for pride or an attitude of *'I know it all'* and *'I have nothing more to learn from you'.* The prevailing spirit in this community is a spirit of teachability. Everyone willing to learn and knowing that there is always more out there.

As a reformer, do you embrace the learning experience through coaches and mentors? Do you have mentors who speak into your life and who pour into you pearls of wisdom? Do you access free and inexpensive learning on educational sites like Udemy and Coursera? It is time to tap into wells of knowledge that you may be the best at what you were designed to do.

A Culture of Action: Let's Do It

This is a call to action. This book is not pie in the sky wishful thinking. No – it is a bold declaration that it is time to take action. It is time to make happen all that we have read. And it has started. That is why you are reading this book. You can hear the sound. I can see the army.

If anything that you read resonated with you, ignited a flame, challenged a belief or motivated you to take certain decisions, then you are part of the growing army. Welcome, Soldier, to the War for the Soul of your Nation.

About the Author

Alero Ayida-Otobo describes herself as a Transformation Strategist with invaluable understanding of sector-wide reforms in Africa. Her close friends call her 'the Original Reformer'. She is passionate about reforming educational and health systems and transforming individuals and institutions. Her burden for education reform began as she served as Transformation Task Team Leader and Adviser to a former Minister of Education in Nigeria.

She was also, for four years, a Lead Specialist for Education Policy under the Education Sector Support Programme for Nigeria (ESSPIN), a programme funded by the United Kingdom Department for International Development (DfID).

A graduate of Oxford University, Bartlett School of Architecture and Town Planning, University of London and the London Business School, Alero's purpose is to *'create wealth in Africa through the development of Human Potential'.* She is currently CEO of Incubator Africa, a development agency operating on the African continent that mobilises and equips Africans to collaborate and actively participate in strategic reform activities. She has worked in different sectors in Nigeria and Ghana and delivered papers at conferences in Uganda, Kenya and Rwanda.

In the summer of 2016, Alero decided to segue into writing. During a sabbatical in California, she completed her first book *Reformers Arise.* The book's sole objective is to activate a people of dignity and integrity whose vision is to change the African narrative. Alero loves to travel and has a deep sense of adventure that has taken her to nearly all the continents of the world with a few exceptions like Australia and the North Pole. She has three beautiful children whom she fondly calls her 'Treasures'.

Professional Pages / Contact

Reformers Arise Network (**www.reformersarise.com**)

Incubator Africa (**www.incubatorafrica.org**)

Twitter: **@ReformersArise**

Facebook: **Alero Ayida-Otobo**

About Incubator Africa

Incubator Africa is an organisation set up by passionate Africans for Africa. We believe it is time to become deliberate in our efforts to bring each part of the region into a place of sustainable development, able to provide a better quality of life for its citizenry.

Africa's greatest wealth is its people. Between 2035 and 2050, Africa's population is expected to reach 2 billion people, out of which 60% is expected to be below the age of 25. No other continent in human history has ever been geared up with such a fantastic force in terms of human capital.

Our response as a social development agency is to intentionally mobilise and equip Africans with the character and relevant skills needed to reform and improve outdated systems and structures in critical areas like Education and other areas that affect human life like Health, Government, Media and Business Development. Our desire is to realise the dream of developing undaunted, relentless Reformers.

We believe this is the time to make this happen. We have created specific capacity development programs for reformers through our Incubator Africa Education Hub - a prototype state-of-the art Centre for Transformation. Our 'Big Hairy' Goal is to foster the growth of a powerful, efficient and effective community of Reformers intent on becoming fully fledged Transformers.

www.incubatorafrica.org

Facebook: Incubator Africa

References

Introduction

Page xxiii: **Collier, Paul** (2007) *The Bottom Billion: Why the Poorest Countries are Failing and What Can Be Done About It,* Oxford University Press.

CHAPTER 1

Page 4: **Sunday Adelaja** is the founder and senior pastor of the Embassy of God, one of Europe's largest churches, in Kiev Ukraine. He is the author of over 80 books. See: ***sundayadelajablog.com***

Page 4: Keynote address by the Vice-President of Nigeria, **Professor Yemi Osinbajo** at the Annual Dinner of Apostles in the Market Place (AiMP) on 20 February 2016.

Page 5: **Mother Teresa** (1910-1997) was a Roman Catholic nun who devoted her life to serving the poor and destitute around the world. She spent many years in Calcutta, India where she founded the Missionaries of Charity, a religious congregation devoted to helping those in great need. In 1979, Mother Teresa was awarded the Nobel Peace Prize and has become a symbol of charitable selfless work.

Page 6: **Gladwell, Malcolm** (2002) *The Tipping Point: How Little Things Can Make a Big Difference*, Back Bay Books.

Page 12: **Martin Luther King Jr** *I have a Dream* is a public speech delivered by American civil rights activist Martin Luther King Jr during the March on Washington for Jobs and Freedom on 28 August 1963, in which he calls for an end to racism in the United States and called for civil and economic rights.

Page 12: **Winston Churchill** said these famous words in his speech made on 29 October 1941 to the boys at Harrow School, a leading boys' school in the United Kingdom. See *The Complete Speeches of Winston S. Churchill*, edited by Robert Rhodes James (1974).

Page 13: **William Kamkwamba** (born 5 August 1987) is a Malawian innovator, engineer and author.
www.en.wikipedia.org

CHAPTER 2

Page 15: **Caine, Christine** (2012) *Undaunted: Daring to Do What God Calls You to Do,* Zondervan.

Page 15: **Caine, Christine** (2014) *Unstoppable: Running the Race You were Born to Win,* Zondervan.

CHAPTER 3

Page 27: **The British Broadcasting Corporation** (BBC) is the world's oldest national broadcasting organisation and the largest in the world by number of employees with over 20,950 staff in total.

Page 30: See ***www.alueducation.com***

Page 36: **Lee Kuan Yew** (2000) *From Third World to First: The Singapore Story 1965 – 2000,* HarperCollins Publishers Inc.

Page 36: the article is published on the *www.educlusterfinland.fi* website.

Page 40: **Sahlberg, P** (2011 and 2015) *Finnish Lessons: What can the World learn from Educational Change in Finland?*

CHAPTER 4

Page 43: **Hybels, B** (2012) *Courageous Leadership, Field Tested Strategy for the 360 Leader,* Zondervan.

Page 45: See *www.mo.ibrahim.foundation.org*

Page 47: **Nicky Gumbel** is an Anglican priest and author. He is also known as the developer of the Alpha Course. See *wn.m.wikipedia.org*

Page 47: **Former United States President, D. Dwight Eisenhower** – see *www.eisenhower.archives.gov*

Page 52: **Former United States Secretary of State, Colin Powell** *www.azquotes.com*

Page 52: **Pope Paul VI** *www.integratedcatholiclife.org*

CHAPTER 5

Page 60: See the **ESSPIN** (Education Sector Support Programme in Nigeria) website for important reports and reviews generated by this programme *www.esspin.org*

Page 61: **Collins, Jim** (2001) *Good to Great: Why Some Companies Make the Leap and Others Don't,* Williams Collins.

Page 61: **Gladwell, Malcolm** (2008) *Outliers: The Story of Success,* Little, Brown and Company.

Page 62: **Raymond Hightower's** blog *10,000 hours of practice* *www.wisdomgroup.com*

Page 67: **Bossidy, Larry and Charan, Ram** (2011) *Execution: The Discipline of Getting Things Done,* Random House Business Books.

CHAPTER 6

Page 77: **The A21 Campaign** exists to abolish injustice in the 21st century. This is a non-profit organisation that believes human trafficking can end. See *www.a21.org*

Page 83: See Quotes on Time and Life – **Sunday Adelaja's** blog *www.new.sundayadelajablog.com*

Page 85: **May Ellen Mark** was an American photographer known for her photojournalism/documentary photography, portraiture and advertising photography. Died 25 May 2015. See *www.maryellenmark.com*

Page 86: **Cunningham, Loren** (2001) Daring to Live on the Edge: The Adventure of Faith and Finances, YWAM Publishing, US

Page 87: **Enlow, Johnny** (2008) *The Seven Mountain Prophecy: Unveiling the Coming Elijah Revolution*, Creation House, Charisma Media.

Enlow, Johnny (2009) *The Seven Mountain Mantle: Receiving the Joseph Anointing to Reform Nations*, Creation House, Charisma Media.

Enlow, Johnny (2015) *The Seven Mountain Renaissance: Vision and Strategy through 2015*, Whitaker House.

CHAPTER 7

Page 95: See **Patricia Hagemann** 'Humility on Hope in the Night' Facebook blog post 7 July 7 2015.

Page 99: **Premuzic, Tomas and Sanger, Michael** (May 2016) *What Leadership Looks Like in Different Cultures*, Harvard Business Review.

CHAPTER 8

Page 102: **Hindmarsh, Bruce** (1997) *William Wilberforce and the Abolition of the Slave Trade: A Gallery of Aristocratic Activists,* article published in Christianity Today.

Page 104: **Silk, Danny** (2009) *Culture of Honor: Sustaining a Supernatural Environment,* Destiny Image.

Page 110: **Swaniker, Fred** – www.alueducation.com. Also TEDGlobal 2014 Talk: *The Leaders who Ruined Africa, and the Generation Who Can Fix It.*

Page 110: **Williams, Rotimi** in www.forbes.com (June 2016) *Meet the 35 Year Old Entrepreneur Who Owns Nigeria's 2nd Largest Rice Farm*

Testimonials

Nothing prepared me for the amazement I would receive as I read this book. I was stunned by the brilliance of Alero's introduction and then it only grew as the book continued. *Reformers Arise* is a clarion calling up – to the whole continent of Africa. Most of the wisdom in this book is needed far beyond Africa and I strongly recommend it for anybody with a heart for reformation of their nation.

Johnny Enlow, *Author/Speaker/Reformer*

Alero Ayida-Otobo has written a brilliant book that hits at the core of who is a true reformer; the qualities that exemplify one; the process of personal development necessary for every true reformer and the need for a new generation of reform-minded individuals to arise. *Reformers Arise* is a practical tool for equippers and the equipped. I highly endorse the book and the author.

Obii Pax Harry, *Apostolic Leader, Resurrection Life Assembly, Birmingham United Kingdom and Nehemiah Apostolic Resource Centre, Abuja Nigeria*

Alero Ayida-Otobo finally writes a book that captures the insights and values that have challenged and inspired a generation of reformers and change makers.
This is a much-needed contribution to shaping the next generation of African leaders.

Gori Olusina Daniel, *Partner Advisory Services,*
Adams and Moore and Chief Inspiration Officer,
World Changers Foundation

This is an insightful, masterful and beautifully crafted book that's not just a manual for young reformers but a guide to a life of integrity, purpose and impact at any age. It is concise and well thought out. Alero's voice is erudite, the style makes for easy reading, and the tone is inspirational yet challenging.
I love this book and can honestly say it's one of the best books I've read in a long time.

Dr Toju Chike-Obi,
Paediatrician, Clinical Director and Host of the HealthZone

The author has a style that is fresh and vibrant. Her passion and delivery is clear and concise. The message is very strong, yet can be read with ease.

Enuma Chigbo, *Publisher and Media Consultant*

Reformers Arise is a tool, a manual, a mandate and a dictionary for reform.
Embrace the truths you will discover within the pages of this great book.

Toyin Matthews, *Ebenezer Care Missions,*
Political Aspirant Senate, Federal Republic of Nigeria

Lightning Source UK Ltd.
Milton Keynes UK
UKHW02f1257060118
315655UK00005B/80/P